SEVEN
The Number of Creation

SEVEN
The Number of Creation

DESMOND VARLEY

G. BELL & SONS
London
1976

First published in 1976 by
G. Bell & Sons Ltd
York House, 6 Portugal Street
London WC2A 2HL

ISBN 0 7135 1947 9

© Desmond Varley 1976

BF
1623
P9
V35

Printed in Great Britain by
The Camelot Press Ltd
London and Southampton

Contents

1	The Septenary	*page* 1
2	The Ternary	29
3	The Quaternary	43
4	In the Beginning....	53
5	Counting and the Practical Uses of Numbers	61
6	The Centre and the Circle	84
7	Involution and Evolution	94
8	Manifestations, Symbols and Practical Uses of the Number Seven	119
9	From Phenomena to Philosophy	146
	Appendix 1: The Constant Elements of the Creation Myth	154
	Appendix 2: The Antediluvian Patriarch List	170
	Bibliography	174
	Index	175

1
The Septenary

Ask a dozen people in succession to name any number between one and ten quickly and the answer you will get in at least eight out of the twelve cases is 'Seven'. This response is so automatic that, when the person being questioned knows the result you expect and so deliberately tries to give a different number, he stumbles and hesitates in his efforts to overcome his own mental 'set'. The number seven is planted firmly in the sub-conscious of the average man as a special number which is somehow different from all the rest.

Its significance is not only a sub-conscious matter, for if a man is offered the choice between two lottery tickets, one of which is numbered seven and the other thirteen, he will almost invariably choose the former, however long he may deliberate about it. There are, of course, individuals who will make a show of their independence in these circumstances by choosing the ticket numbered thirteen, but such people are acting in a spirit of conscious bravado and are aware that they are 'flying in the face of providence'. Their overt actions have to overcome a great deal of internal resistance.

It is easy to say that this attitude is simply the result of 'superstition' but the label does not explain the fact. Whatever name we give to the condition, we are forced to admit that pure number does have a definite effect upon our thinking and therefore on our lives.

The book is the result of an attempt to find out why. We chose the number seven as the centre around which our investigation revolved because, of all the numbers, it has had the greatest symbolic significance for humanity in all ages and in all parts of the world.

It was Hippocrates who said, 'The number seven, because of its occult virtues, tends to bring all things into being; it is the dispenser of life and the source of all change — for the moon itself changes its phase every seven days. This number influences all sublime beings.'

The Pythagorean school most of all developed the idea that number was the basic stuff of the universe. The notes of the musical scale, the colours of the rainbow, the march of the stars across the heavens, the body and the mind of man, time and eternity, all could be explained as the interaction of number upon number.

Yet it can be argued that number cannot exist without the objects to which it refers. There is no such *thing* as three: there can only be three eggs in a basket or three men in a boat. Seven, as an object, does not exist; there can only be seven notes in the diatonic scale or seven days in the week. How, then, can pure number, which is simply an *idea*, not a tangible thing, influence anything at all?

The Idea of Number

When we discuss pure number, we are in the realm of ideas, rather than that of concrete things. The pure mathematician tends to look down from his lofty mental heights with something like disdain on the man who puts his formulae to practical uses. His researches are detached completely from what most of us regard as the world of reality; he is concerned only with the beauty of the patterns created in his mind by the logical operations he performs with his symbols.

A number is such a symbol, although the bulk of pure mathematics has progressed beyond the 'number fields' to those of thought itself. One of the basic processes of modern mathematics is that of generalisation, by which, first particular numbers, then types of numbers and, finally, the idea of number, are progressively removed from every problem, until the mathematician is left with pure form or pattern, into which number can intrude only as a special case.

The idea of number is itself, strictly speaking, the idea of order or pattern. In its simplest form, it is seen as the division between unity and plurality. Before we can speak of *two*, we must have the concept of *one*. To form this concept, it is necessary to transcend the mental limitations imposed on our thinking by the manifold forms of the physical universe. We cannot simply raise one finger and say 'This is one', because we are thereby involved in the thought that this particular finger is part of a set of ten and we could have raised any one of the other nine to make the same statement. To think of One, pure and undifferentiated, we have to anihilate the world in thought and try to imagine the primeval state before the process of creation began. At first glance, we may feel that we have now reduced everything to a state of nothingness and so we might be tempted to write the figure '0' as a description of the state in place of the figure '1' which we want to use, but this is a false assumption because we have, in imagination, taken the place of the Creator; the mind which is now imagining the state is itself the One which remains when the Many is absorbed.

In this way, we are able to give meaning to the unity which is the basis of all numbers. The One is that which exists in itself, complete and whole, without polarity. It is that which has no opposite. When all else is gone, it alone *is*. It contains within itself all potentiality, but in its pure state cannot be said to have any qualities at all. If this sounds like a mystical description of God, we are in good company, because Pythagoras insisted that One was the number of the Almighty.

The one to which we point when we raise a single finger is a pale reflection of the basic concept which we have tried to convey. The One contains the potentiality of the Many within itself. This is to say that plurality is necessarily of a lower order than Unity; the single finger I raise to denote 'one' is of the *same order* as my other nine fingers.

How is plurality produced from unity? Bearing in mind the concept of Unity which is our starting point, we cannot say that One is duplicated to make two, for where does the second come from? Again, we have to usurp the position of the Creator in imagination. The process of creation, we find, can only be one of *division*. Within the undifferentiated One must arise polarity. 'Light must be separated from darkness'. Thus the undifferentiated becomes the differentiated; the One becomes two, and yet the two remain united in the One. Each of the polarised partners created by the process has a unity of its own, but it is a unity of a lower order than that of its Creator; it is the unity of *separation*, not that of *completeness*.

It can therefore be seen that the idea of number is really the idea of the separation of *this* from *that*, but it also implies that the individual members of a number-set are related to each other and are capable of being re-absorbed into their original unity. We can only add three cats to four dogs if we first agree to combine the terms 'cat' and 'dog' in a term of a higher order, in this case 'animal'. The addition then becomes 'three animals plus four animals is seven animals'.

It will be noted that it has already become necessary to depart from the idea of pure number and attach numbers to objects. To get back to number in itself, we have to think of the *pattern* formed by the objects in space and time, but leaving blank spaces in the imagination in the positions which the objects should occupy. It is possible to 'feel' the rhythm of the waltz without mentally humming a particular tune and, by analogy, it is possible to visualise the order and pattern of number without attaching number to particular objects.

In this sense, we can think of number in itself as order and process and we can say, for instance, that the number seven influences man and his universe if they tend to arrange themselves into patterns, rhythms and sequences which are typical of that number.

Man is created in the image of God because he, like God, is a unity, but man's unity is of a lower order than that of God, because he holds it at the expense of separation from his fellow-men. Nevertheless, his unity, or selfhood, enables him to comprehend the patterns of plurality, so that pure number has a meaning for him.

The Pattern of the Septenary

Pure number can be considered as order *or* pattern. These terms relate to arrangements in either space or time. A spatial arrangement is a geometrical figure, while a temporal arrangement is a rhythm.

The pattern of the septenary with which we are most familiar is temporal, the rhythm of the seven-day week, which affects all our lives. We go to church on Sundays, start work on Mondays, visit the cinema on Tuesdays, play golf on Wednesdays, entertain our friends at home on Thursdays, get paid on Fridays and watch cricket on Saturdays. The pattern is repeated week after week with small variations so that the seven-day rhythm is as much a part of us as the daily rhythm of waking and sleeping.

This rhythm is not, however, limited to man in our particular society. Each phase of the moon takes seven days to complete and there is a seven-day period between neap tide and spring tide and again between spring tide and neap tide. This suggests that the origin of the rhythm is lunar.

Darwin thought that the reason why the human female follows a menstrual or lunar cycle was that man's ancestors originated in the sea and that one effect of the tides had been to impress their rhythm on human physiology. The objections to this theory are: first, that the menstrual cycle has *twice* the period of the tides and secondly that other creatures which are also believed to have descended from sea-dwellers do not obey a similar rhythm, their periods of heat and fertility being related more closely to the solar seasons than to those of the moon. Nevertheless, the synchronising of the rhythms of the moon

THE SEPTENARY

and of the human female must have had awesome significance for the men who first observed it.

The seven-day week is the only form of the septenary which has any practical mundane significance for modern man, all its other uses being related to folk-lore, superstition or religion. It is therefore all the more surprising that the number itself still carries the same aura of magic for us that it did for our ancestors. It is the *symbolic* significance of the number which is important rather than its practical use.

It has been the invariable habit of number-symbologists to refer the number seven to the seven 'planets' known to the ancients, each of which is associated with one of the gods of the Roman pantheon. These are the sun and the moon plus the five 'naked-eye' planets, Mercury, Venus, Mars, Jupiter and Saturn. The present writer believes that the sacred quality of the number developed *before* it became attached to the planetary gods, this attachment being a later, but quite natural, extension of the number's symbolism. Before discussing such theories, however, we shall examine the traditions of the number's planetary associations.

The Alchemical View

It is to medieval alchemy that we must first turn in examining the relationship of the planetary gods to the number seven. The alchemists were visibly engaged in such activities as the transmutation of metals, but they themselves believed that the Great Work was really performed on their own natures, transmuting the mundane consciousness into something higher. For this reason, they used the materials of their visible work as symbols. Each of seven metals was associated with one of the planetary gods and correspondences were traced between the physical properties of the metals and the spiritual qualities represented by the gods. Their list of planetary correspondences is given in the following table:

PLANETARY GOD	ASSOCIATED METAL	PLANETARY GOD	ASSOCIATED METAL
Sun	Gold	Mars	Iron
Moon	Silver	Jupiter	Tin
Mercury	Mercury	Saturn	Lead
Venus	Copper		

The alchemists' symbol for the septenary nature of the ladder of the metals was this curious sign:

In a medieval treatise in which the sign appears, it is explained that the circle or globe represents the essential unity of matter, the cross and square allude to the four directions of space and the four elements of which matter is composed: earth, water, air and fire, while the triangle signifies the three principles of creation.

It is significant that the alchemists themselves were divided on the question of the number of separate processes which were necessary to complete the Great Work. Sometimes the number was given as seven and at other times as 12; only these two numbers appear in this connection. Now while it is true that these numbers are those of the days of the week and the months of the year respectively, the numbers also arise from two ways of combining the numbers three and four shown in the symbol, one being the result of adding and the other of multiplying. It seems obvious from this that more importance was attached to the idea of combining the numbers three and four than to the resulting numbers themselves.

The idea underlying the Great Work is seen to be that of creation. The alchemists were trying to imitate the Creator and so were consciously following what they believed to be the pattern of the processes of creation. The description of the symbol shows that they conceived this pattern to be one in which three creative principles result in four created elements, which are combined in varying proportions in all matter. We shall see that this division of the septenary into a higher ternary and a lower quaternary is a factor which is explicit or implicit in many of the septenary's symbolic uses.

The Seven-day Week and the Gods

How often, when a man says 'I'll see you on Thursday', does he give any thought to the god to whom the day is dedicated, Thor, the Norse god of thunder? Most of us are vaguely aware of this dedication of each of the days of the week, but there is rarely an occasion when we need to stop and consider how and why the individual days became the 'property' of the seven gods.

In the names of the days as they have come down to us in English, there is a curious mixture of Germanic, Norse and Roman gods. It is necessary to examine the names in several languages before the correspondences between the English names and the gods of the planets become apparent.

Sunday. No difficulty here. The day is clearly dedicated to the sun-god.

Monday. Again, we do not need a dictionary to tell us that this day is dedicated to the moon. In French, it is *Lundi* (from *la lune* – the moon), while Spanish has *Lunes* and German *Montag*.

Tuesday. From the Anglo-Saxon *Tiwdaeg*. Tiw was the Scandinavian god of war. He was also known as Tyr, Dis or Dings, hence the German word for the day is *Dienstag*. The Romans associated Tiw with their own god of war, Mars, and this connection is shown by the Spanish and French names for the day, which are *Martes* and *Mardi* respectively.

Wednesday. This is Woden's day. Woden was the West Germanic form of Odin, the Nordic god who replaced Thor as the leader of the gods. His appeal was to the intellectuals whereas that of Thor was to the peasants. Odin resembles the Egyptian god Thoth in his main characteristics. Thoth was known to the Greeks as Hermes Trismagistus and was the direct equivalent of the Roman Mercury. This is no coincidence, for we find when we examine the name of the day in French and Spanish that Wednesday is dedicated directly to Mercury in these languages (French – *Mercredi*; Spanish – *Miércoles*).

Thursday. Thor's day. Thor was, of course, the Nordic god of thunder. In German, the day is *Donnerstag* (thunder day). The Roman equivalent was Jupiter or Jove and this is the god commemorated in the French and Spanish names of the day, *Jeudi* and *Jueves*.

Friday. From the Anglo-Saxon *Frigedaeg*, the day of Frigga or Freya*, the wife of Odin and the Norse goddess of love and fertility.

---

*Frigga and Freya were recognised as two separate goddesses originally, but the similarity of their qualities and names suggests a single original. In any case, they were, later, often treated as one goddess.

She is equivalent to the Roman Venus and we shall not be surprised to find that in French the day is named *Vendredi* and, in Spanish, *Viernes*.

Saturday. Straightforward again; it is the day of the Roman god, Saturn, the god of animal husbandry, later to be identified with the Greek Kronos, who signified the passage of time.

There is therefore no doubt that the days of the week are dedicated to the seven planetary gods:

>   Sunday to the sun   Thursday to Jupiter
>   Monday to the moon   Friday to Venus
>   Tuesday to Mars   Saturday to Saturn.
>   Wednesday to Mercury

The Gods of the Week

(1) THE SUN

It is natural that the first day of the week should be dedicated to the chief of the gods, for such the sun-gods invariably are. Probably the first divine being to be worshipped is the Earth-mother, from whom man has sprung and who gives birth to everything that lives. Her worship, however, is not of something remote and awesome. She has an image which is closer to that of a human mother than of a true goddess. To some extent, man is able to influence her directly, by tilling the soil, for instance. It is only when he looks beyond his immediate surroundings and begins to speculate about the heavenly bodies that he steps into the region of the unknown and, therefore, awesome.

The sun influences his life for good or evil and there is little he can do to counteract or change that influence except to make sacrifices, the smoke of which he hopes will rise up to the sun-god and please him so that he may show mercy.

This is the god who is born anew each day and who passes through the underworld each night, who may one day provide pleasant warmth, the next day parching heat and on the next day may withdraw completely behind the clouds, leaving man at the mercy of the cold.

In the ancient temple of Ra at Heliopolis (the city of the sun), known to the Egyptians as On, the central object was the *ben-ben*, a sacred pyramid-shaped polished stone. This stone was the symbol of the sun-god himself, being the solidified form of the sun's rays spreading out on to the earth. The pyramid was chosen as the shape of the tomb of the pharaoh because the pharaoh was identified with the god and the pyramid is the sun-symbol. However many gods the Egyptians possessed, the supreme creator was the god of the sun, Ra.

If the pyramid is a three-dimensional symbol of the sun, its equivalent in two dimensions is a golden disc with rays radiating from the centre. It is significant that early Christian art used this symbol in the form of a halo or nimbus to identify the head of Christ in paintings or stained glass. In Mal. iv, 2, Jesus is referred to as the *Sun* of Righteousness.

It is not surprising that Sunday became the sacred day of the Christians. The Gospel narrative asserts that Christ was crucified on the day which we call Friday and rose from the dead on the first day of the week, i.e. Sunday, but it is entirely possible that this circumstance was inserted into the tradition by the early promoters of the religion in order to provide a direct correspondence between Christ and the sun, to whom the first day of the week is dedicated. In this way, they could take advantage of the existing traditions of the solar religions and redirect their fervour towards the Lord of Christianity.

'In theogony,' says Cirlot in his *Dictionary of Symbols*, 'the sun represents the moment (surpassing all others in the succession of celestial dynasties) when the heroic principle shines at its brightest. . . . On occasion, the sun appears as the direct son and heir of the god of heaven, and Krappe notes that he inherits one of the most notable and moral of the attributes of this deity: he sees all and, in consequence, knows all.' This image tallies in detail with the image of Christ as the centre of the Christian religion and it is small wonder that the Christian fathers should want to make use of the sun symbolism.

In most religions, the sun can be discerned as the 'all-seeing eye' of heaven. It is symbolic of death and resurrection in its daily setting and rising, a sequence which is repeated by the moon every month and by the seasons every year, the theme of which is the core of almost every religion.

In alchemy, the sun is associated with the most noble of the metals, gold, partly because of the correspondence of their colours, but also because the sun is recognised as the highest visible symbol of deity.

Psychologically, the sun is the symbol of the active, masculine principle, imparting life to whatever it touches. There is in the choice of Sunday as the sacred day of Christianity an interesting contrast with the Sabbath of the Jews. The latter is the day on which God rested and on which man must do the same. The principle is entirely passive while that of the Christian day is entirely active. This is not the whole story, however, for we recognise a 'divine paradox' in the sun-symbol; the sun is the only body which is at rest in relation to the planets of the other days of the week. It is the centre of the whole system and remains in its place while the others rush around in their orbits. So the sun is the symbol of the 'mysterious Centre', the Source of all manifestation, the One which creates the Many, unmoved and unmoving but never ceasing Its creative activity.

This image is archetypal in the sense in which Jung used the term. As a symbol, it has the power to evoke from the subconscious a response which has nothing to do with rational thinking but which influences directly the thoughts, emotions and activities of the human being.

(2) THE MOON

The moon provided the second unit of time which man used to mark off the periods of his life. The solar day is the most obvious of the rhythms by which he lives, but it loses its usefulness as a time-marker when dealing with longer periods of time. And so, the phases of the moon provided him with a more convenient longer unit, the month, later to be divided into four weeks corresponding to the four distinct phases.

Cicero remarked that 'every month the moon completes the same trajectory executed by the sun in a year'. It also repeats symbolically the four seasons of the year and its cycle may thus be considered as a 'little year'.

The symbolism of the moon is essentially feminine. It is the passive receiver of the creative light of the sun. Its connection with the female cycle gives it, by analogy, an influence on fertility, even in the vegetable kingdom. Its connection with the tides also has a correspondence with the waters of the womb and its phases suggest the changes in appearance of a woman during pregnancy.

The moon's feminine associations are ambivalent; they have both a good and evil aspect. Diana and Hecate are both lunar deities. From a psychological standpoint, this situation probably arises because, while the moon gives light, it does not destroy the darkness of the night. The light in which it bathes the world is pale and mysterious and it leaves large areas in frightening shadow, so that, while it is the light *par excellence* of lovers, it is also the light of felons and evildoers. Of all the heavenly bodies, the moon is the one most closely associated with the activities of imagination and dreaming.

(3) MARS

Tiw and Mars are gods of war. In this day and age, we can no longer subscribe to the idea of the glory of war; war is to us mere senseless killing. There is, however, a sense in which war is a necessary principle of creation. What is created in time must be destroyed in time and it may even be said that it is the continuous battle between the forces of manifestation and dissolution which maintains the tensions on which existence depends. The glory which was ascribed to the more civilised wars fought by our forebears related to the nobility of sacrifice. The man who would sacrifice even his life for what he saw as his duty was considered as being only a little lower than the gods, for sacrifice is a *creative* act. The seed is sacrificed under the earth to give life to the plant. Christ is sacrificed on the Cross to give life to humanity.

In this sense, the god to whom the third day of the week is sacred represents the third member of a divine trinity. The first two members, the sun and the moon, signify the polarising principles (masculine-feminine, active-passive, positive-negative), while Mars represents the principle of reaction between them.

It is not insignificant that many of the greatest benefits of civilisation have been created as a result of war. The greatest technological advances have almost invariably taken place in response to the need for new offensive or defensive weapons in wartime. War stirs up all the forces of civilisation from the bottom, and the outcome is the most intense creative activity alongside the most thorough destruction.

Tension is necessary to life. If a man is enabled to live completely without tension, he will become a vegetable, unable to bestir himself to any form of creative activity. Think, for instance, of the millions of men who spend their lives competing with their fellows for the better jobs, more money, a bigger share of the market and similar individual goals in commerce and industry. A very large proportion of these men are looking forward with keen anticipation to the day when they can retire from the 'rat-race' and enjoy life. But when retirement comes, many of them just fade away and die, for when there is nothing more to fight for, there is nothing more to live for.

The Mountain of Mars has twin peaks; they represent the opposing poles of dualism. It is the function of Mars to control the interaction of the two poles; his war is what prevents them flowing together and mutually anihilating each other.

(4) MERCURY

If the first three days of the week are sacred to the divine principles of activity, passivity and reactivity, the fourth relates to the first of the 'lower' or human attributes, intelligence or perhaps, at a higher level, wisdom, for this is the primary feature of Mercury.

The Greek name, Hermes, signifies 'interpreter' or 'mediator' for he was not only the messenger of the gods but also the arbiter of their disputes. The planet Mercury is the lively planet because its position in the sky varies rapidly, and so the god is pictured as a messenger with wings on his feet, rushing to and fro between the other gods. This attribute is also reflected in the metal mercury or quicksilver, which, being in the form of a heavy liquid, is very difficult to grasp and, if held in the palm of the hand, darts to and fro.

The planet alternates between being an evening and a morning star and so the nature of the god is held to be duplex. Mercury is hermaphroditic (Hermes plus Aphrodite), a combination of both masculine and feminine characteristics, and represents both 'good' and 'evil' forces. While he is the god of wisdom, he is also the demon of sophistry and 'double-dealing'.

For Jung, he represents the *anima*, or feminine principle, in a man and the *animus* of a woman, both of which have to be assimilated and accepted by the conscious individual before complete self-integration, or to use Jung's own term, 'individuation', can occur.

(5) JUPITER

Thor in Nordic mythology, like Jupiter in the Roman, is the god of thunder. Both are strong, brutal and have gross appetites. Jupiter or Jove gives us the word 'jovial', which describes an individual who enjoys the satisfaction of his sensory desires to the full.

Thursday, then, is sacred to the god who represents the gross physical nature of man. At the abstract level, he is brute force or will, the second of the four necessary attributes of man, that part of his nature which enables him to *act*.

The fact that Jupiter is the father of Mercury (as Thor is the father of Odin) signifies that, in man, the will-to-act precedes the wisdom to act rationally. The picture presented is one of a blind force, irresistible but undirected. It needs the direction of intelligence (Mercury) and the motivation of emotion (Venus) to channel it into purposeful activity. Without these two, it is pure animal; with them, it becomes human.

(6) VENUS

Venus is the prototype of a feminine deity in a man's world. She is the successor to, but does not displace, the Earth-mother goddess, who is the product of a matriarchal society. The Earth-mother image arose naturally when man began to form settled communities and to till the soil. The analogy between the productivity of the earth and the child-producing function of woman was too obvious to be missed by primitive man, but it was the status of woman as head of the tribe which provided, by extension, the impetus for the actual *worship* of the Earth-mother. Fertility without emphasis on sexuality was her main characteristic. Gradually, however, as the male began to take over the dominant role in society, the character of his goddesses changed. The sexual element was recognised as a causal factor in fertility and this element took over as the primary attribute of the goddess.

Venus is therefore woman *seen through man's eyes*. She is the ideal of beauty and is at the same time wanton, representing the typical dream-object of man's sexuality. She is depicted as arising naked from the foam of the sea, as in the case of her Greek counterpart, Aphrodite. No other image could show her origins so clearly, for the sea is the archetypal symbol of both the womb and the subconscious; its foam typifies the production of dreams, and the arisal of the goddess is a faithful picture of the way the sexual element is often explicitly presented in dream material. It must be concluded that Venus is the projection of man's sexuality.

Far from being a reason for minimising the worship of the goddess, this background actually intensifies it, for this is the one form of worship with which a man can identify himself body and soul. The very word 'veneration' means 'the act of doing what is done to Venus', for the worship of Venus carried more fervour than that of all the gods put together. No other religion, even the strict monotheism of the Hebrews, could stamp it out, hence the many references in the Bible to the evils of the worship of Ashtoreth, the Phoenician version of Astarte, who is identified with Venus.

Venus was worshipped in many different guises. Primarily, she was the goddess of beauty and sensual love. The wife of Vulcan, she still gave her favours to Mars and many other gods. She was the mother of Cupid by Mercury. As Venus Verticordia, a temple was founded to her by three Vestal Virgins in reparation for having lost their virginity. The founding at Rome took place on April 1, 114 B.C. and thereafter April 1 became the Veneralia, her chief annual festival. As Venus Genatrix, she was worshipped as the goddess of marriage and motherhood, while as Venus Victrix, she was represented as the goddess of victory on Roman coins.

The girdle of Venus (or Aphrodite), made by Vulcan, carried the magical power of generating ardent love for the wearer in any man she desired. It fell off her while Mars was making love to her and was left on the Acidalian Mount.

The planet Venus has similar feminine characteristics to those of the moon. The brightest and most beautiful of the true planets, she is seen in phases similar to those of the moon and, like Mercury, she alternates between being a morning and an evening star. Like the goddess, therefore, the planet signifies both the fertility and the fickleness of woman.

The human attribute characterised by Venus, to whom Friday is dedicated, is the capacity for emotion, that which drives a man on to accomplish his most exalted, as well as his most depraved, deeds. Without this emotional drive, man achieves nothing, but unless emotion is directed and controlled by intelligence and will, it can run away with a man, resulting in the perversion of his aims. Venus represents both sublime love, seen as the fulfilment of man's highest aspirations in which he 'rises above himself', and pure lust, which is destructive, self-directed body-love.

(7) SATURN

Like his Greek equivalent, Kronos (from whom we derive our words 'chronic', 'chronology' etc.), Saturn symbolises time, which devours all things. For this reason, he is supposed to have devoured his own children except Jupiter (representing air), Neptune (water) and Pluto (the grave), which are proof against time.

Saturday is therefore directly related to the day which follows it, Sunday, for the former represents the inevitability of death, while the latter refers to the possibility of resurrection or new life. We use the word 'saturnine' to describe someone who is grave, gloomy, phlegmatic, as though he were looking his own death in the face. The colour associated with Saturn is black, the colour of death.

The Roman Saturnalia, celebrated each year in December, was the ritual acting out of the idea of succession, the death of the god to ensure the continuation of the line, in a parallel to the succession of earthly kings. Frazer has noted that a man was elected annually to represent Saturn and, for the days of the festival, was given all the honours and privileges due to the god. At the climax of the rite, he was either assassinated or committed suicide. During the Saturnalia, no business could be transacted and the operations of the law were suspended, including the punishment of malefactors. The direct successors of the central figure in the Saturnalia in Europe in the Middle Ages were the 'Abbot of Unreason' and the 'Lord of Misrule', whose festivals included the blatant suspension of all rules of decency, with orgies and debauchery taking place even within the walls of the great cathedrals. The clergy themselves did not hesitate to take part in these festivals, even to the extent of celebrating mock masses. It was as if all were acting out the principle of 'eat, drink and be merry for tomorrow we die'.

The motivating principle of such inversions of ordinary existence is the desire to intensify all the experiences of life for a brief period, to realise the essence of earthly life in preparation for its extinction.

As the fourth attribute of man, Saturn signifies man's inextricable placement in time and space. This is the source of his mortality – as man – since immortality, being outside of space and time, is a divine, not a human, attribute.

We can thus see that, in the order in which they appear in the days of the week, the planetary gods exhibit the three-four dichotomy suggested in the alchemical interpretation. The three principles of creation, signified by the sun, moon and Mars are the active, passive and interactive principles, while the four 'elements' of man are: intelligence (Mercury), will (Jupiter), emotion (Venus) and mortality (Saturn).

The Genesis Creation Story

The Genesis story of the creation follows a similar pattern. The sequence may be summarised as follows:

The first day, God created light, separating it from darkness.

The second day, He created the vault of heaven, separating the waters above from the waters below.

The third day, He created dry land, by separating it from the lower waters, and spread vegetation upon it.
The fourth day, He created the sun, moon and stars.
The fifth day, He created the fish, sea-monsters and birds.
The sixth day, He created the animals, reptiles and man.
The seventh day, He rested.

In this account, the first three days are devoted to the creation of the 'fields' in which the creatures of four subsequent days are to have their activities.

The connection between the light and darkness of the first day and the *symbolic* sun (as opposed to the physical sun mentioned on the fourth day) is obvious. This is the light of consciousness, which is the first principle of creation, in relation to man.

The separation of the waters by the vault on the second day has clear allusions to the tidal effects of the moon and so embraces the lunar symbolism already described. This separation also refers to the unconscious.

The significance of the third day's creation is more elusive. The creative divisions of the first two days are clear-cut; light is separated from darkness and the two are mutually exclusive; the upper and lower waters are separated and kept far apart by the vault. The separation of land and sea of the third day is a different case, for the two remain joined at the shoreline. What is more, from the moment of their creation, they are destined always to be at war with each other, with the sea constantly eroding away the land and the silt from the land, having been brought down to the sea by the rivers, constantly filling up the sea's bed. Here we have the warring principle of Mars acting as a creative force, for it is the interaction of the water (rain) and the land (soil) which is the necessary background for the appearance of vegetation, here symbolising the diffuse principle of life.

In relation to the interpretation of the first two days' creations as consciousness and the unconscious, depth psychology tells us that these two areas of mental activity are constantly at war with each other; that which is consciously repressed, for instance, remains in the unconscious until it finds the opportunity to force itself to the surface in another form. This process is inevitable and can only be reconciled by assimilating into consciousness the images of the unconscious which seek expression. A special creative activity of the mind is called for to bring order and destroy the 'demons' which might otherwise cause psychoses.

So we interpret the first three days of creation in their aspect relating to the mind of man as being the three principles of consciousness, the unconscious and the reaction between the two. In their cosmic aspect, the three principles are activity (the 'outgoing' principle of light), passivity (the 'incoming' principle of water) and reactivity (the warring principle of land and sea).

Now we come to the 'lower' elements of creation which arise from the 'higher' principles.

The fourth day produces the heavenly bodies. At the physical level, this refers to the material universe, the concretisation of the pure Form which was pre-existent at the spiritual level. In relation to the psyche of man, it signifies the appearance of intelligence, which operates through an appreciation of the world as it sees it. Rational thinking has to use concrete symbols (the heavenly bodies) instead of pure Form, with which it has no means of coping. As Mercury is the interpreter of the gods, man has to interpret the symbols shown to him by the universe. Astronomy was the first science, well-known to the Babylonians who gave to the Hebrews the material on which the Genesis story of creation is based. The sun, moon and stars are then a reference to science as an interpreter of the universe.

On the fifth day, fishes and birds appear. The text specifically refers to the 'monsters' of the sea. This is a reference to the Thor-like nature of man as his animal instincts would make him. The birds refer to the unbridled passions released in physical man which, uncontrolled, must result in the libertine, gratifying every lust where he wills.

On the sixth day, first animals and reptiles and then man himself are created. Man is given dominance over the other creatures and told to go out and multiply. Sex is mentioned for the first time – 'male and female He created them'. Man is created in the image of God, but it is significant that he is created on the same day as the animals. This refers to his dual nature, animal and divine. He is to multiply and rule over the rest of creation. The symbol of sexual union here relates to the *conjunctio oppositorum*, the reconciling, in this case, of the animal and the divine, through which man may become whole. This, too, is the symbolism of Venus. She is the Love which reconciles all opposites and enables man to become complete – animal and divine – a physical and spiritual whole.

Having achieved this state, God and man rest on the seventh day. This cessation of activity is not conceived as death in the sense of anihilation. The darkness of Saturnalian death is not the same as the

		THE WEEK OF	
	SUNDAY	MONDAY	TUESDAY
DAY-GOD	SUN	MOON	TIW
ROMAN	SOL	LUNA	MARS
GREEK	HELIOS	SELENE	ARES
GENDER	MASCULINE	FEMININE	MASCULINE
METAL	GOLD	SILVER	IRON
COLOUR	YELLOW	WHITE	RED
GENESIS	LIGHT AND DARKNESS	VAULT SEPARATING WATER	LAND AND SEA
MATTER	ACTIVE	PASSIVE	ORDERING
LIFE	CONSCIOUSNESS	SUB-CONSCIOUS	INTERACTION
CREATIVE GROUPS	TERNARY		
	THE TRINITY OF CREATIVE PRINCIPLES		

darkness of primeval chaos. It is simply the end of the 'wars of Mars' brought about by complete integration. Thus, the whole Man can say 'I am in the world, but not of it ... for I have conquered the world.' And as Sunday follows Saturday, the death of one level of activity, brought to completion, is followed by the possibility of resurrection at a higher level to begin the work of creation anew. Man is mortal, but possesses immortality potentially.

So we see that there is a close correspondence between the pagan symbolism of the gods to whom the days of the week are dedicated and the biblical story of creation. The correspondence is too close to be coincidental.

THE SEPTENARY

CREATION			
WEDNESDAY	THURSDAY	FRIDAY	SATURDAY
WODEN	THOR	FREYA	SATURN
MERCURY	JUPITER	VENUS	SATURN
HERMES	ZEUS	APHRODITE	KRONOS
HERMAPHRODITE	MASCULINE	FEMININE	MASCULINE
QUICKSILVER	TIN	COPPER	LEAD
PURPLE	BLUE	GREEN	BLACK
CELESTIAL BODIES	FISH AND BIRDS	ANIMALS AND MAN	REST
AIR	FIRE	WATER	EARTH
INTELLIGENCE	WILL	EMOTION	MORTALITY
QUATERNARY			
THE DOUBLY-POLARISED ELEMENTS OF CREATED MATTER			

Symbolic Lists
The septenary is the normal form into which lists of abstract qualities are moulded. We shall not be surprised to find that the 'three-four' pattern is commonly repeated in such lists.

There are thus seven natural sciences, divided into the Trivium (Grammar, Logic and Rhetoric) and the Quadrivium (Arithmetic, Music, Geometry and Astronomy). Similarly, the seven virtues consist of three Supernatural Virtues (Faith, Hope and Charity) and four Cardinal Virtues (Prudence, Justice, Temperance and Fortitude). The seven Deadly Sins are divided into three sins of the mind and four of the body. They are: Pride, Wrath, Envy, Lust, Gluttony, Avarice and Sloth.

The Roman Catholic Church recognises seven divinely-instituted sacraments, of which the first three relate to the spiritual life while the remaining four are directed towards mundane life. The sacraments are: Baptism, Confirmation, Eucharist, Penance, Orders, Matrimony and Extreme Unction.

The Lord's Prayer begins with an invocation and ends with a dedication. The substance between these ritually-normal parts of the prayer consists of seven petitions, of which the first three are God-directed and the last four man-directed:

Petition 1 — May Thy Name be hallowed
Petition 2 — May Thy Kingdom come
Petition 3 — May Thy Will be done on earth as in heaven
Petition 4 — Give us this day our daily bread
Petition 5 — Forgive us our trespasses as we forgive others
Petition 6 — Lead us not into temptation
Petition 7 — Deliver us from evil

In the Mohammedan religion, the number seven occupies as prominent a position as it does in the religion of the Jews. The Mohammedan tradition of the Garden of Eden tells how God sent three archangels — Gabriel, Michael and Israfel — one after the other, to find seven handfuls of earth of different colours with which to create Adam. Each in turn came back empty-handed. Finally, Azrael was dispatched on a similar errand and, having completed his mission successfully, was appointed to be the Angel of Death from that time for ever.

The expression 'to be in the seventh heaven of delight' comes from the Mohammedans, who recognise seven distinct heavens.

The first heaven is of pure silver. It is the abode of Adam and Eve and in it all the stars — each with its attendant angel — are hung on golden chains like lamps.

The second is made of pure gold and is the abode of John the Baptist and of Jesus.

The third, of pearl, is the domain of Joseph. In this heaven, Azrael, the Angel of Death, continuously writes and erases the names of human beings in a great book.

In the fourth heaven, of white gold, the domain of Enoch, the Angel of Tears never ceases to weep for the sins of men.

The fifth heaven is made of silver and is the dwelling place of Aaron and of the Avenging Angel who presides over elemental fire.

The sixth, of ruby and garnet, is the home of Moses. It is presided

THE SEPTENARY 21

over by the Guardian angel of Heaven and Earth, who is half snow and half fire.

The seventh is the 'real' heaven of indescribable divine light. It is the domain of Abraham and it is said that here each inhabitant is bigger than the whole earth and has 70,000 heads, each with 70,000 faces, each face having 70,000 mouths, each with 70,000 tongues, each speaking 70,000 languages and all are continuously engaged in chanting the praises of the Most High.

Both the Christians and the Mohammedans inherited their uses of the number seven from the Hebrews, for whom the seven-branched candelabra is a sacred symbol. It was, of course, the Jewish Cabalists of the Middle Ages who carried Hebrew number symbolism to such lengths that some men devoted their whole lives to its pursuit. Like the Mohammedans, the Cabalists recognised seven heavens, each succeeding one being more full of happiness than the one below it; the seventh was the abode of God and the highest class of angels. The seven celestial hierarchies of the Cabala are connected with the seven planetary spheres as in the following list, which also shows the presiding archangel in each case:

1. The Sun, with the Angel of Light, Michael.
2. The Moon, with the Angel of Hope and Dreams, Gabriel.
3. Mercury, with the Civilising Angel, Raphael.
4. Venus, with the Angel of Love, Anael.
5. Mars, with the Angel of Destruction, Samael.
6. Jupiter, with the Administering Angel, Zachariel.
7. Saturn, with the Angel of Solicitude, Oriphiel.

The canonical books of the Bible mention only two of the angels of the Cabala, Michael and Gabriel. The Apochryphal Book of Enoch (viii, 2) gives the seven holy angels as Michael, Gabriel, Raphael, Uriel, Chamuel, Jophiel, and Zadkiel, the first three being the same as those of the Cabala, while the last four are different.

The Old Testament naturally abounds with references to the number seven, most of which are connected directly or indirectly with the six days of creation and the seventh day of rest.

In Genesis 7,2, Noah is told to take into the ark seven pairs of all ritually-clean animals and birds and one pair of those which are not clean. Curiously, the story goes on to relate that Noah took with him only one pair of both clean and unclean animals and birds. On the face of it, Noah disobeyed the command of the Almighty. Since there is no other comment on the point, however, it must be assumed either that there is a scribal error involved or that the tradition itself was mutilated before it was even written down.

Pharaoh's dream, which was the medium of Joseph's elevation in Egypt, concerned seven fat cows and seven lean cows; seven full ears of corn and seven thin ears.

The main feasts of the Hebrews are of seven days' duration and the most important sacrifices are ordained to consist of seven animals. The idea of the Sabbath is applied to agriculture in Leviticus 25,1. For six years, the Hebrews may sow and reap, but in the seventh year, the land is to lie fallow. Similarly, after each period of seven times seven years, a year of jubilee is proclaimed. This is the source of our own use of jubilee celebrations during the fiftieth year of a reign or the existence of some organisation. It has nothing to do with the idea of a half-century, but is the year after the completion of seven times seven years.

In Numbers 22, when Balaam, the seer, is asked by Balak, the king of the Moabites to bring down the denunciation of the Lord on the Israelite army, Balaam asks for seven altars to be built and seven rams sacrificed on each altar. The results being unsuccessful, the procedure is gone through three times on different sites before Balaam finally predicts the overthrow of the Moabites by the Israelites.

At the fall of Jericho, described in Joshua 6,1, the army marched round the walls of the city on six consecutive days once each day, preceded by seven priests with seven trumpets. On the seventh day, they marched round the walls seven times, after which the seven trumpets were sounded and the army raised a great shout. As a result of this procedure the walls of the city collapsed. The story is a clear indication of the magical use to which the Hebrews put their sacred number. Essentially, the number is connected with the idea of creation, but here we see it being used magically to bring about destruction.

It is a pity that Proverbs 9,1, which mentions the seven pillars of wisdom, does not say what they are. The poetic context quite obviously assumes that they were well-known symbols and it is possible that they consisted of a list of virtues similar in character to the seven virtues with which we are familiar. According to Psalm 111, the *beginning* of wisdom is 'fear of the Lord' and this may have been the first of the seven pillars.

There is a particularly interesting piece of symbolism in Zechariah

THE SEPTENARY

Wisdom hath seven pillars

3,9, which reads:

> *Here is the stone that I set before Joshua, a stone in which there are seven eyes. I will reveal its meaning to you; says the Lord of Hosts. Then I asked the angel of the Lord who talked with me, 'Sir, what are these?' And he answered, 'Do you not know what these mean?' 'No, sir,' I answered. 'These seven,' he said 'are the eyes of the Lord ranging over the whole earth.'*

In this passage, the number seven signifies completeness. Seven eyes are sufficient to cover the whole earth.

In the New Testament, there is less stress on number symbolism, but it is noteworthy that, in one of the versions of the story of the miracle of the feeding of the five thousand by Jesus, the disciples started with seven loaves and when the people had eaten, there were enough scraps to fill seven baskets. (In the other account there are five loaves but 12 basketfuls).

Acts 5,2 describes how seven officials were appointed by the twelve Apostles to look after the material welfare of their followers. We shall see later that there is a significant connection between the numbers twelve and seven quite apart from their reference to the months of the year and the days of the week.

In the Book of Revelation, the number seven occurs 54 times. It is not clear whether the number is used for its own symbolism or simply in relation to the seven churches to which the Book is addressed. Since the whole Book is a mass of symbolic numbers, however, including the cryptic 666, the Number of the Beast, it is probable that the seven churches themselves were chosen for their number to represent the whole of Christendom.

The most potent testimony to the veneration with which the number seven was regarded by the Hebrews is the etymology of the Hebrew verb 'to swear', which means literally 'to come under the influence of seven'. In connection with swearing, Herodotus (111, viii) describes an Arabian method of oath-taking which involves seven stones being smeared with blood.

It is certain that the symbolic use of the number seven was not an original idea of the Hebrews themselves. Some 2500 years before the Christian era, a Sumerian king, Lugulamnemundu, built a temple to the goddess Nintu at Adab. The temple had seven gates and seven doors and, at its dedication, seven times seven animals were sacrificed, showing that the ancient Sumerians themselves considered the number to be sacred.

In Classical Greece, the number had an exalted status. The lyre of Orpheus had seven strings and it was Pythagoras who was credited with discovering that the frequencies of the seven notes of the diatonic scale in music are related by small integral proportions. There were seven Hesperides, seven sons and seven daughters of Niobe, seven kings who attacked Thebes and seven who defended it.

Ranging further afield than the fertile belt which is the cradle of Western civilisation, we find in Japanese folklore seven gods of luck. These are: Benten, the goddess of love; Bishamon, the god of war; Daikoku, the god of wealth; Ebisu, the god of self-effacement; Fukurojujin and Jurojin, both gods of longevity; the Hstei, the god of generosity. These gods are related to the seven Buddhist Devas who are said to be responsible for the welfare of humanity.

According to Cola Alberich, the 'fox with seven tails' is the evil genius of the Chinese, among whom it is traditional that the saints and sages have seven holes in their hearts. On the seventh day of the seventh month, great popular festivals were held all over China. The Chinese also hold the lotus with seven petals to be a magical amulet similar to our four-leafed clover.

Buddhist scriptures use number-symbolism very extensively. In his book, *Myths, Dreams and Mysteries*, Mircea Eliade draws attention to a significant use of the number seven in a Buddhist text.

THE SEPTENARY

As soon as he is born, the Bodhisatva places his feet flat on the ground and, turning towards the north, takes seven strides, sheltering under a white parasol. He looks at the regions all around and says, with his voice like that of a bull, 'I am at the top of the world; this is my last birth; for me there will never again be another existence.'

This description must, of course, be read with the aim of Buddhism in mind, which is to escape from the 'wheel of existence' representing the many painful rebirths implied by the doctrine of reincarnation. The interesting part of the theme, from the point of view of our present investigation, is the idea that the world is transcended by going through seven stages, represented by the seven steps. Professor Eliade automatically associates these stages with the seven *planetary* heavens. In common with most authorities, he assumes that the origin of the significance of the number is to be found in the planets.

The Hindus, no less than the Buddhists, regard seven as a sacred number. The Prajapatis, the mind-created children of Brahma, number seven and there are seven Rishis or sages and seven Manus, or rulers of the world, each reigning for a Manvantara. (14 Manvantaras are equal to one Kalpa, which is a period of 12,000,000 divine years, each consisting of 360 ordinary years.)

In Hindu thought, man is conceived as existing on seven planes: those of Sensation, Emotion, Reflective Intelligence, Intuition, Spirituality, Will and Intimations of the Divine. This leads to the esoteric conclusion that there is a direct correspondence between the spheres of activity of man and the seven planetary spheres.

It may or may not be significant that when the ancient Mayas first organised their very exact and comprehensive calendar system, they chose as the starting point of their chronology a date which was seven *baktuns* before their own time, a *baktun* being a period of 400 years of 360 days each.

In Peru, there exist ancient Indian pyramids in which the *guaca*, or tomb of the sun, always has seven steps.

It is doubtful whether the modern usages of the number seven have independent origins. In most cases, they are consciously or unconsciously following the precedents set by our ancestors. The wonders of the ancient world are seven, not because there were no others, but simply because, when the number seven was reached, it constituted a 'complete' number and this was the obvious point at which to stop listing. The 'seven seas' fall into a similar category because, in order to make the number up to seven, the Pacific and Atlantic are arbitrarily divided into North and South. Presumably, Rome had more than just seven hills, but we only hear about the Palatine, Capitol, Aventine, Caelian, Esquiline, Viminal and Quirinal.

Shakespeare's seven ages of man are equally arbitrary and the age of 21 at which a man is said to attain maturity was probably chosen *because* it was three times seven. The Romany idea that the seventh son of a seventh son is gifted with clairvoyance sounds like folklore turned into a good 'sales gimmick' for itinerant seers!

The reputed seven colours of the rainbow constitute a slightly different case. The fact is that the number of colours in the rainbow is as large as we like to make it, because the gradation of hues is continuous throughout the spectrum and we can divide it anywhere we like. If we use the commonly-recognised and named colours to describe the rainbow, we shall say that it starts with red, which fades into orange, then into yellow, green, blue and violet. These colours number *six*, not seven. Another colour, indigo, has been inserted between blue and violet to make up the sacred number. Except when it appears in the rainbow list, we normally think of indigo as 'one of the blues'.

Nevertheless, as we shall now proceed to show, there is a sense in which the number of visible colours, not counting black and white as colours, is seven. This arises from a peculiarity of human vision by which three colours are seen as pure and all the rest as mixtures, a circumstance which allows books to be printed in full-colour using only three colours of ink.

If we examine again the six rainbow colours, we find the following:

Red is seen as a pure colour. We cannot see it as a mixture of other colours.

Orange is readily seen as a mixture of red and yellow.

Yellow is again a pure colour.

Green is seen as a mixture of yellow and blue.

Blue is a pure colour.

Violet is seen as a mixture of blue and red.

In this list, we have three pure colours and three colours which are each mixtures of two of the pure colours. There is just one other possible way of mixing three pure colours and that is *to mix all three together*. As anyone who has worked with primary colours in pigments

THE SEPTENARY

knows, this combination produces the seventh basic colour, *which is not part of the rainbow spectrum at all*, but which is one of the most common colours on earth, *brown*.

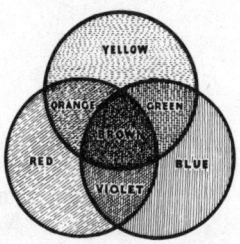

The seven colours which result when pigments of the three primary colours are used together. Each of the large circles is presumed to be filled with a primary colour, which mixes with the others where the circles overlap.

It can be seen, therefore, that the origin of the seven colours is a matter of simple mathematical combination. Starting with three primary colours, we add all the possible ways of combining them and find that four new colours are added, making seven in all. The number of individual colours is as large as the human capacity to differentiate between them but *all* colours can be made by combining the three primary colours in varying proportions. Nevertheless, ignoring different proportions of the same combination, there are only seven ways of combining them; three in which a primary colour is used alone, three in which two primary colours are mixed together and one in which all three are combined. This fact was discovered by ancient man almost as soon as he began to decorate his caves with pigments.

It will not have escaped the reader's notice that this pattern of colour-mixing provides a rational background to the already-noted dichotomy of the symbolic number seven into two parts, with the numbers three and four attached to them. The ternary of primary colours is seen to be of a 'higher order' than the quaternary of mixed colours. The principle applies to any form of creation-by-manipulation which starts with three basic elements. If we have three elements, A, B and C, there are exactly seven possible ways we can set them out, singly or in combination:

> A
> B
> C
> AB
> AC
> BC
> ABC

In 'mixing' the elements above, we were not concerned with the order or structure of the mixture but only with the ingredients. If we decide that the order in which the elements appear in a mixture is to count, then exactly 12 ways exist of mixing the three pure elements, four in which A appears first, four in which B appears first and four in which C appears first:

> AB   AC   ABC   ACB
> BA   BC   BAC   BCA
> CA   CB   CAB   CBA

2
The Ternary

We have shown that the symbolic septenary usually contains two separate parts, with three and four elements respectively and that the ternary section usually refers to a 'higher order' than the quaternary. We must therefore look at the ternary on its own to see what common features are exhibited by its various symbolic uses.

In ritual, to repeat an action or phrase three times is to emphasise what is being done or said to the point of irrevocability. 'Holy, Holy, Holy' is a magical repetition designed to *fix* the idea of sanctity both in the mind and in the ritual object.

Sometimes, the three repetitions involve a sort of *crescendo* of emphasis as in the Confession formula; 'My fault, my own fault, my own most grievous fault.' This idea has a parallel in the story of Peter's denial of Christ. The first time he was asked whether he was one of those who had been with Jesus, he simply denied it; the second time, he denied it on oath and the third time, he denied it with a 'penalty-oath', the strongest form of denial a Hebrew could make, thus committing himself completely and irrevocably.

Three is the invariable number of times a cult-action was to be repeated in ancient Egypt – again a method of impressing the symbolic act on to the ritual object to the utmost degree.

To the Pythagoreans, three was the perfect number because it had a beginning, a middle and an end. For similar reasons, it was the symbol of Deity as Creator.

The god of the Brahmins was represented with three heads and the Brahmins themselves wore the Triple Thread from one shoulder to the other to show their dedication to him.

The ancient Greeks had three Fates, three Furies and three Graces, while the Muses were three times three. Gods were often represented with a tripartite instrument of power, e.g. the trident of Neptune and the three-branched lightning of Jove.

The world was visualised by the ancients as consisting of three parts: heaven, earth and the underworld. Therefore, man had also to have three divisions, which became his body, soul and spirit.

Deity as Trinity

The most potent use of the number three is found in the description of Deity as Triune. Sometimes, as in Christian dogma, it is specifically stated that God has three aspects, but is One in essence (Father, Son and Holy Ghost, in this case). In other cases, a triad of individual gods is named and each can be, and is, worshipped separately, although the inner teaching is invariably that these are but three facets of the same Supreme Being.

The second chapter of the Prose Edda, for instance, refers to the Nordic Triad, Har, Janfar and Thridi, meaning the High, the Equally High and the Third. Thridi, in spite of his name, was recognised as the chief of the triad.

The chief triad of the Babylonians consisted of Anu (the sky), who was the chief god, Enlil (the earth), who was the lord of storm, and Ea (water), whose main attribute was wisdom. They also had a second triad: Sin, the moon-god, Shamash, the sun-god, and Adad, the thunder-god. In charge of Meslam, the Babylonian underworld, and completing the triad of triads, were Nergal, the sun-below-the-horizon, Ninmug, the queen of the underworld, and Loz, their co-ruler.

The main triad of the ancient Egyptians was, of course, Osiris, Isis and Horus, typical of a class of triads consisting of father, mother and son.

The Nordic Nornes or Fates were three sisters, named Urd, Verdandi and Skuld, who represented the past, present and future respectively.

The Etruscan triad: Tina, Cupra and Menrva, representing fire, fertility and wisdom, are united by a common symbol of power, the thunderbolt. The gods of the Hindu triad: Brahma, Siva and Vishnu, are worshipped separately by the masses, but one of the earliest lessons taught to candidates for initiation into the inner mysteries is that their separation is illusory and all are aspects of the One. The Buddhists say that the created world is a world of illusion. It is created by three principles, which are Desire, Form and Spirit, and thus the world has three regions or planes: the Kama Loka, or world of desire, the Rupa Loka, or world of form, and the Arupa Loka, or world of spirit.

Among the North American Indians, many of the tribal stories of the Deluge tell how life was recreated, after the flood subsided, by a mother and a pair of twin sons, one of whom is conceived as good and the other as evil. A similar idea is inherent in the creation legend of the Zoroastrians, which says that, in the beginning, there existed Anahita, the mother-goddess, Zervan-Akarana, the principle of good, and Ahriman, the principle of evil.

Chinese creation myths say that matter was formed from chaos, which divided itself into the male and female principles, Yin and Yang. From these sprang a giant named Pan-Ku, from whose body came forth the visible world. Ya Chi'o Miao said that man had three souls: his shadow, his reflection in water and his real self. This echoes the Egyptian view that man consisted of a Ba or soul, a Ka or double and a Khaibit or shadow.

Jung contends that the psyche of a man *acts as if* it consists of a conscious self, plus a 'shadow' – his double in the unconscious which impells him to realise his repressed ideas and is thus his 'evil' counterpart – and the *anima*, which represents the female elements in a man and, like the 'shadow', is an apparently autonomous archetypal image operating in the region of the unconscious.

The Forces of Creation

The meaning of the three-gods-in-one is thus quite plain and it is from this meaning that the number three receives its symbolic significance. It is that the process of creation – and, therefore, the nature of both God and man – is threefold. Three is the number of the forces of creation. The character of these forces is represented as a pair of opposites plus an interacting factor. This idea is best exemplified by the triad which consists of a good and evil pair plus the mother-goddess.

We are now reaching an area of thought in which symbol is a very thin cloak for truth. To approach the underlying principle, we shall turn to some of the basic ideas of mechanics which are familiar to most schoolboys in the higher grades.

Forces acting on a body, e.g. gravity, magnetism etc., may be represented by vector arrows in which the direction of the force is shown by the direction of the arrowhead and its strength by the length of the arrow. We imagine, for instance, a coin resting on a smooth table-top which is level. Two forces are acting on the coin: the force of gravity is pulling it vertically downwards with a certain strength and the reactive force exerted by the table-top itself is pushing it upward with equal strength. The two forces exactly balance each other so the coin is in equilibrium and does not move.

This state of affairs is represented by vector arrows of the same length pointing upwards and downwards from the position of the coin.

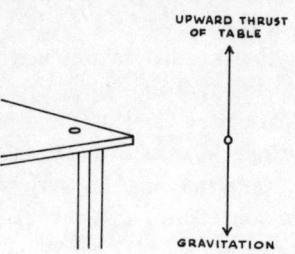

If we now tip the table to an angle of 45 degrees, we shall destroy the equilibrium of the coin. The force of gravity will still be acting vertically downwards, but the thrust of the table-top will now be at an angle of 45 degrees to the vertical, thus:

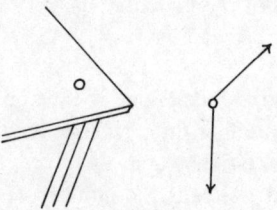

Experience tells us that the coin will now slide down the sloping surface as if a force were pushing it from some direction to the left of the vertical. This hypothetical force is the *resultant* of the other two forces and its strength and direction may be shown diagrammatically by constructing a parallelogram on the two original vector arrows and then using the diagonal as the resultant vector.

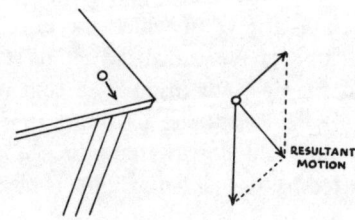

THE TERNARY 33

In order to restore equilibrium to the coin, we can apply a *third* force, equal and opposite to the resultant (by pushing the coin in the direction of the upward slope of the table-top). This leads to the concept of a *triangle of forces*. In this triangle, the oblique force exerted by the table-top and the vertical force of gravity are represented by vector arrows which form two sides of a triangle, while the resultant (A) or the single force necessary to restore equilibrium (B) are represented by another vector arrow forming the third side of the triangle.

A little thought will show that when all the arrows go the same way round the triangle, we know we are dealing with a state of equilibrium.

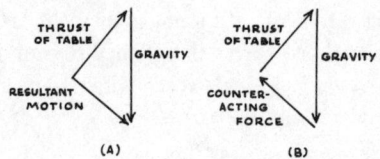

Now let us see in what way this arrangement is analogous to the supposed principles of creation.

We have to assume as our starting point the primeval state before the material universe emerged. This state is symbolised by the number One and is equivalent to God-in-Himself, the Undifferentiated Source of being. This is a state of perfect equilibrium in which all potentiality exists but in which nothing *happens*. In creation myths, it is often referred to as Chaos, but the modern connotations of this word, suggesting a picture of a meaningless maelstrom, give a wrong impression of the state. The term 'Void' may be better if we bear in mind that the Void is still the source of plenitude.

Now the first step in the creation process is the arising of polarity within the previously undifferentiated Void. This is symbolised by the separation of light and darkness. In terms of our mechanical diagram, we can represent the Void as a point. The appearance of polarity will then be represented as two equal vectors pointing downwards at right angles to each other.

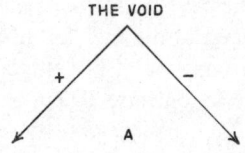

34 SEVEN, THE NUMBER OF CREATION

If we put a hypothetical observer at point A in this diagram, he will look towards the right and left and see two equal and opposite principles, one of which will attract and the other repel him. From his point of view, one of the arrows should point in the opposite direction to that shown above. For example, if we equate the arrow marked by a plus-sign with 'good' and the one marked by a minus-sign with 'evil', we must change the 'plus' arrow to point upwards 'in the direction of goodness', while the other continues to point downwards 'in the direction of evil'. Note that, in this analogy, the change of direction is really an illusion of the observer. If he were able to put himself in the position of the Creator, he would see both arrows as pointing downwards. However, once we look at the emanations of the Source 'from the outside' we have to deal with them as they *appear*. And so we arrive at the classical triangle of forces in which the resultant of the upward and downward arrows is a single force which appears as an attraction towards the downward-pointing arrow.

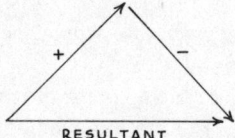

As long as this state of affairs continues, there can be no state of equilibrium, but there will be a continuous flow from, let us say, the 'good' towards the 'evil'. A third force is therefore necessary to restore equilibrium, equal and opposite to the resultant of the first two, so that our completed diagram looks like this triangle, into which a compensating force has been introduced, operating towards the 'good'.

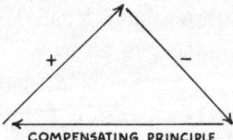

This is the third principle of creation, which enables a sort of equilibrium to be maintained in the manifestations of the Creator. We say 'a sort of equilibrium' advisedly, because *complete* equilibrium is never attained in the material universe. There is always some under- or

THE TERNARY

over-compensation, which results in continuous change or flux — a state of *becoming* rather than of static *being*.

This idea of the triune nature of the creative principle has been, from time immemorial, basic to Hindu philosophy. The three principles are known to the Hindus as the *gunas* and it is said that anything which exists, materially or in the mind, is created by an admixture of the three *gunas*, the only difference between two things or ideas being the proportions in which the *gunas* are combined.

In an appendix to Christopher Isherwood's translation of the *Bhagavad Gita*, he describes the *gunas*:

> *Pakriti* is said to be composed of three forces, known as the *gunas*. They are *sattwa*, *rajas* and *tamas*. During the 'night of Brahma', the phase of potentiality, these *gunas* are in a state of perfect equilibrium and *Pakriti* remains undifferentiated. Creation is the disturbance of this equilibrium. The *gunas* then begin to enter into a vast variety of combinations, corresponding to the various forms of differentiated mind and matter. Their characteristics may be known from their products in the psychic and physical worlds.
>
> In the physical world, *sattwa* embodies all that is pure and fine, *rajas* embodies the active principle and *tamas* the principle of solidity and resistance. All three are present in everything but one *guna* always predominates. For example, *sattwa* predominates in sunlight, *rajas* in an erupting volcano and *tamas* in a block of granite.
>
> The *gunas* also represent the different stages in the evolution of any particular entity. *Sattwa* is the essence of the form to be realised; *tamas* is the inherent obstacle to its realisation; and *rajas* is the power by which that obstacle is removed and the essential form becomes manifest.
>
> In the mind of man, *sattwa* expresses itself psychologically as tranquility, purity and calmness; *rajas* as passion, restlessness, aggressive activity; *tamas* as stupidity, laziness, inertia. Sometimes one *guna* is predominant, sometimes another; and a man's mood and character vary accordingly.

In reading this description, one may gain the impression that *sattwa* is 'good' while *tamas* is 'bad', but this is not the view of the Hindu. In themselves, the forces have no moral implications and may work towards either good or evil quite indiscriminately. For instance, in order to persevere in any undertaking and to resist the temptation to turn aside from the path he has set himself to follow, a man makes use of *tamas* combined with *rajas*.

Nevertheless, the Hindu believes that, in the evolution of a man, he will progress from the predominance of *tamas*, through that of *rajas* to that of *sattwa*. But this is not the end of the evolutionary road; he must now progress beyond even *sattwa* to that state in which all the forces are transcended.

This Hindu insight, ages old as it is, is an unassailable analysis of both mind and matter. If we look closely, we shall find that the same idea is expressed or implicit in all the great religions of the world. In Christianity, it is the symbolic import of the Holy Trinity; the Father represents the Almighty in His aspect as *sattwa*, that which provides order and law in the universe; the Son represents *tamas*, God-made-flesh, i.e. matter; and the Holy Spirit represents *rajas*, the driving force which keeps the universe in motion.

The symbolic content of the triads which are found in many other religions may not always be as evident as in the case of the Christian Trinity, but it seems as if the Rule of Three is one of those ideas which arises spontaneously in all cultures and is therefore a subconscious recognition of the way creation functions.

Folklore carries an immense volume of references to the ternary nature of man and the universe. Perhaps the most obviously symbolic use of the number three is the three wishes given to a mortal by a supernatural being in many fairy stories. The pattern is so consistent as to suggest that all the varieties come from a single original source. The mortal makes his first wish, which is granted, but once he has the thing he has asked for, he is dissatisfied with it and makes a second wish, which is also granted, with a similar result; the third wish is either made inadvertently or is forced upon the mortal by the granting of the second, but, either way, it has the effect of cancelling out whatever has already been obtained. The Hindu would say that this represents the evolution of the psyche through successive lives. First, a man may be living the life of *tamas*, but, eventually, he will long to break out of his prison and will become a man of *rajas* and, later, of *sattwa*, from which state he will glimpse the unreality of all these differentiated states and return, at last, to the Real, which transcends them.

The triune nature of God with respect to His creation gave rise to the use of the equilateral triangle as the symbol of Godhead. Tradition-

THE TERNARY

ally, this triangle stands on its base and has one angle pointing directly upwards, presumably towards 'that which is above'.

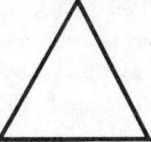

This is opposed to the representation of that which is created, for which a similar triangle is used with its angle pointing downwards.

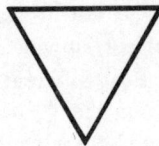

Their combination in the so-called Seal of Solomon signifies, for the Jew, the Law of God and the necessity for His creatures to follow it to the letter.

In Judaism, most traces of references to a Trinity have been expunged because of the Jew's religious fear of idolatry. It must be remembered that the early history of the Jews is one of a struggle to maintain their national identity as they moved among other nations and, later, as their own land was taken over as part of the Roman empire. This struggle is the prime incentive for their thoroughgoing monotheism, which contrasted so strongly with the many gods of the Romans in the immediate pre-Christian era. It is probable, however, that in spite of the removal of the Rule of Three from official, popular religion, the initiates of the priesthood were taught some form of it as a secret doctrine which set them apart from the common man. Almost all the known Hebrew names of God are tri-syllabic, including, we believe, the name represented by the sacred tetragrammaton — Yod, Heh, Vaw, Heh — which was not permitted to be pronounced aloud by any Jew except the High Priest and even he could only pronounce it once a year. This name is today rendered as *Yahweh* by most authorities in contrast to the older accepted form of Jehovah. However, when the Heh occurs in the middle of a word, it is quite likely to form a syllable of its own — a *sounded* breathing rather than the silent aspirate with which we are familiar in English.

In the Hermetic tradition, the double triangle is the symbol of the dictum 'As above, so below'. This expression has been given so many interpretations that it may be as well to state its meaning clearly here. It means that there are direct correspondences between the patterns of existence of different creatures at different levels of evolution and that these patterns are imposed upon them in the 'act' of creation. The fact that the double triangle is used to symbolise the idea shows that the basis of creativity in the Hermetic and Hindu traditions is exactly similar. Both are based on the Rule of Three.

Those individuals whose aim is the performance of ritual magic think that the principle of 'As above, so below' can be used for a sort of two-way trade. By means of ritual invoking correspondences between the materials used in the ritual and the magical effect they are trying to produce, they imagine that they can perform miracles. The best-known example is the rite in which pins are stuck into an image representing an enemy. Crudely expressed, theory suggests that this will cause the person to be harmed as he would if sharp instruments were stuck into him. Now I am not going to claim that the victim is never harmed in such a case. Witchdoctors *are* sometimes successful. What I do suggest is that it is the concentrated *intention* in their own minds which produces the effect, not the correspondences with the ritual actions, which only serve as a focus for their mental concentration. The gods are not influenced by the petty actions of man. From their positions high on the spiral of evolution, they can see the futility of the things which seem so important to a mere mortal!

'As above, so below' represents the correspondences which are an inseparable aspect of creation, not the willy-nilly influence of one level of existence on another and certainly not the influence of the 'lower' on the 'higher'.

THE TERNARY

The word 'spiral' was used above deliberately. The spiral is the symbol of the evolutionary process. The reason for its use is that, in evolution, history is said to repeat itself but that each repetition occurs at a higher level. An evolving entity, let us say, a man, will be confronted with similar patterns of life at different stages of his evolution. His reactions to these patterns will vary according to whether he has profited from his previous similar experiences on the lower arms of the spiral.

The spiral is therefore a representation of the cycles of time. When no further evolution is possible, the spiral becomes a simple circle, the sign of eternity or that which is outside time. Both the spiral and the circle are often graphically shown by the image of the serpent. In its coiled form, the serpent represents time and evolution, but when it appears as a complete circle, with its tail in its mouth, it represents eternity.

In Genesis, the serpent is the evil influence responsible for the 'fall' of man. This fall consisted of his eating of the Tree of Knowledge. Now the story surely cannot mean that God wanted to keep man in a state of perpetual ignorance, although this is certainly the surface meaning. What is more, the knowledge concerned seems to be sexual in character, for Adam and Eve only 'discover their nakedness' after eating the fruit. Again, this does not tie up with God's previous injunction to go out and multiply. The Eden story must therefore either be taken as it stands but entirely symbolically or it must be read as a corruption of an earlier story, the scribe who reproduced it being ignorant of the meaning of the symbols he was using. Let us assume the former circumstance and examine the sequence of the story:

1. Man is created in the image of God.

2. He lives in Eden in perfect contentment.

3. The serpent draws his attention, through the woman, to the Tree of Knowledge and persuades him that he will benefit from eating its fruit in spite of God's injunction that, if he eats of the Tree, he will die.

4. He eats the fruit and 'his eyes are opened'. God is then made to soliloquise that 'the man has become like one of us, knowing good and evil'.

5. He is cast out of Eden and cherubim with flaming swords are put to guard the way to the Tree of Life, the other forbidden Tree in the garden.

Man's creation in the image of God is usually taken to mean that man was created in a form somewhat like that of God. It is possible that a quite different meaning is intended. Creative thinking produces mental images and it is sometimes said that the whole created universe exists only in the mind of God. If this meaning is attached to the biblical account, then God is simply inserting man into the image of the universe already created in His mind. If, on the other hand, we use the conventional interpretation, we must assume it to mean that man was created with a mind which functions on similar lines to the mind of God. Why, then, does he have to eat of the fruit of the Tree before he 'becomes like one of us, knowing good and evil'? We know that, in the beginning, the man was living in Eden in perfect contentment, with nothing to fight for and apparently with no knowledge beyond the mere surface appearance of the rest of creation. This is a good description of a man ruled by the first of the three *gunas*, *tamas*. The serpent, signifying the passage of time, makes him dissatisfied with his state and arouses in him the desire for something different, so that *rajas* takes over and he disobeys the command of the Almighty and eats of the fruit of the Tree of Knowledge. The man of *rajas* is said to be distinguished by his thrusting forward to take what he wants from life with complete disregard of the welfare of others. As soon as he has eaten the fruit, his 'eyes are opened' and he begins to see things as they really are. He 'sees his own nakedness', or, in other words, becomes aware that there is more to life than unthinkingly gratifying his own desires. He is able to be ashamed of his own imperfections or, as we should say, develops a conscience. This is a description of a man beginning to be ruled by *sattwa*.

If we read the symbols in this way, the Eden story becomes a description of evolution which tallies in detail with the Hindu viewpoint. We can also read a new meaning into the expression 'in the image of God'. It means that, because the act of creation is a disturbance of the three forces which are the nature of the Creator, created man must also be subject to the same three principles, but out of equilibrium.

Once he has begun to evolve, man is thrown out of the garden into the maelstrom of the rest of creation. He wants knowledge of life, therefore he must suffer, for suffering is the best, often the only teacher.

Why did God forbid man to eat of the fruit in the first place? Actually, 'forbid' seems to be the wrong word, because what God was saying was '*if* you do eat the fruit of the Tree of Knowledge, you will

THE TERNARY

surely die'. This is not a threat, although the scribe makes it appear so; it is a simple statement of fact. A man with no knowledge of life *cannot* die, because there is for him no contrast between life and death and, in this sense, he is immortal. The cabbage cannot grieve because one day it will be eaten! But, as soon as he develops a consciousness of self, which only follows his experiencing some of the meaning of life, he graduates to the ability to die. He then tends to see death as the negation of life. And not until he has transcended all three of the *gunas* is he also enabled to transcend the idea of death, because he is then able to rise above time itself; in biblical terms, the serpent can no longer bruise his heel.

For this state, there is yet another symbol. This is the circle of eternity added to the double triangle representing the Creator and His creation.

Now this symbol is said to represent all that is from the point of view of the Creator. For man, working his way up the evolutionary spiral, the symbol, with one addition, has a different, but analogous, meaning. The addition is a dot at the centre of the design. It represents the mysterious Centre, about which we shall have more to say later.

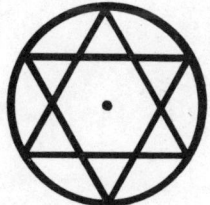

In this form, the symbol is taken to represent man's situation in relation to the eternal. The triangle with its point upward is his 'higher', or spiritual nature, while the triangle with its point downward is his 'lower', or animal nature. Both bear a similar relationship to the circle of eternity, but, between themselves, they are constantly at war because they pull in opposite directions. The Centre is the essence or pure Self of the man and it is said that, when eventually the war between the *apparent* selves is resolved, he will know that his real Self, his Centre, is the same as that of God. As the Hindu scriptures put it, 'the Atman and Brahman are One' or, more succinctly, 'Thou are That'. This is almost the same as the saying of Jesus: 'The Kingdom of Heaven is within you'.

3

The Quaternary

From the earliest times, four has been the number of the physical world, which was composed of four elemental substances: earth, water, air and fire. It derives part of its significance from the four points of the compass.

It may be asked why there should have been just four cardinal points or directions and not three or five or six. The concept is likely to arise naturally as a result of the left-right symmetry of the human body.

When a man stands, he is said to 'face' in a certain direction. The word itself is the clue to the concept. It is the result of the instinctive assumption that *forward* is that direction to which the eyes, and therefore the face, are pointed.

Once we have localised the forward direction, we immediately become conscious of its opposite, the direction which is *behind* us. In the broadest sense, we can now divide the world into two halves, the half which is in front of us and the half which is behind us, but we are faced with a problem almost at once. How do we describe the direction of an object directly to our right? We could say that it is half way between front and back, but an ambiguity is involved in this description; the object *could* be directly to our left, leading to an error of 180 degrees!

It is at this point that the symmetrical structure of the body influences our thinking. We get out of the difficulty by naming the one side after our right hand* and the other after our left hand. As soon as we have done so, all ambiguity of description is removed. If I am facing in the direction of '12 o'clock' and there is an object situated in relation to myself at between one and two o'clock, I can tell you that it

---

*The 'right' hand is distinguishable because most people use it more than the other. It feels *right* to work with and so the other hand tends to be *left* out of activities.

is half way between front and right and you will know exactly what I mean. So four cardinal points are the minimum necessary to enable any direction we choose to be described unambiguously without pointing.

A similar argument may be used to derive four elements from the primeval Void. The Void is first polarised from 'left to right' and these two areas of polarity are again polarised from 'top to bottom'. This process results in a fourfold division, consisting of two polarisations at right angles to each other. Each of the four 'quarters' will now have completely different characteristics.

An analogous division of human psychological types is accepted as a convenient means of classification. The left to right polarity is described as the introversion-extraversion scale, while the vertical polarities are between stability and instability. This results in a diagram such as that shown below, on which any particular personality-type may be shown by a position somewhere in one of the four quadrants of the circle.

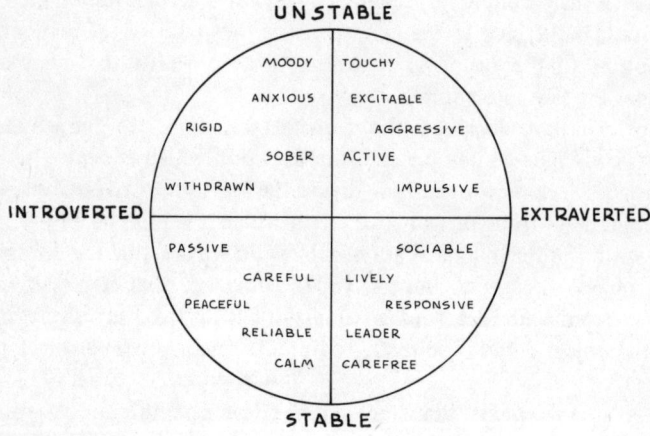

It is in one of these two senses that all symbolic uses of the number four are found.

In the Bible, the number four is not prominent, but we find that the river of Eden splits into four when it leaves the garden. The names of the four rivers are equated with those of Mesopotamia, but the symbolic intention is obviously to indicate the fourfold nature of created matter.

THE QUATERNARY

The sacrificial altar has four horns, which refer to the four cardinal points, while the four beasts around the throne in Revelation have a similar meaning but also refer to the four elements. At the crucifixion, the soldiers divided Jesus' garments into four parts. We shall return to the symbolism of crucifixion, but we note meanwhile that this division of the garments signifies the dissolution of the material body of Jesus and its return to the four elements of which it was composed.

The ancient Mayas had four gods called Bacabs, each of whom was the supporter of one of the four corners of the earth. The gods, together with their points of the compass and their symbolic colours are as follows:

CAUAC	—	SOUTH	—	RED
MULAC	—	NORTH	—	WHITE
KAN	—	EAST	—	YELLOW
IX	—	WEST	—	BLACK

A similar idea is found in ancient Egypt, where Horus had four sons whose images adorned the canopic jars in which the internal organs of embalmed mummies were preserved. Each was the god of one of the cardinal points and the protector of one of the organs. They were:

AMSET	—	SOUTH	—	LIVER
HAPI	—	NORTH	—	LUNGS
DUAMUTEF	—	EAST	—	STOMACH
QEBSNEUF	—	WEST	—	INTESTINES

Thus we find an Egyptian septenary following exactly the pattern we have been describing. Osiris, Isis and Horus are the divine triad representing the three creative principles, while Amset, Hapi, Duamutef and Qebsneuf are the quaternary of created matter.

Four is, of course, the number of the seasons of the year and of the phases of the moon. Presumably by analogy, it is also the number of the named parts of the day: morning, afternoon, evening and night. These time sequences were seen by the ancients to have their counterpart in the life of man, or, for that matter, of any living thing: i.e. birth, growth, decay and death.

In the glossary appended to C. G. Jung's autobiographical work, *'Memories, Dreams and Reflections'*, the following entry will be found under the heading 'Quaternity':

> The quaternity is an archetype of almost universal occurrence. It forms the logical basis for any whole judgment. If one wishes to pass such a judgment, it must have this fourfold aspect. For instance, if you want to describe the horizon as a whole, you name the four quarters of heaven.... There are always four elements, four prime qualities, four colours, four castes, four ways of spiritual development etc. So too, there are four aspects of psychological orientation. In order to orient ourselves, we must have a function which ascertains that something is there (sensation); a second function which establishes *what* it is (thinking); a third function which states whether it suits us or not, whether we wish to accept it or not (feeling); and a fourth function which indicates where it came from and where it is going (intuition). When this has been done, there is nothing more to say.... The ideal completeness is the circle or sphere, but its natural minimal division is a quaternity.
>
> A quaternity or quaternion often has a 3 plus 1 structure, in that one of the terms composing it occupies an exceptional position or has a nature unlike that of the others. (For instance, three of the symbols of the Evangelists are animals and that of the fourth, or St Luke, is an angel). This is the 'Fourth', which, added to the other three, makes them 'One', symbolising totality. In analytical psychology often the 'inferior function' (i.e. the function which is not at the conscious disposal of the subject) represents the 'Fourth' and its integration into consciousness is one of the major tasks of the process of individuation.

The two accepted symbols of the quaternary are the square and the cross. As a sacred symbol, the cross antedates the Christian era by thousands of years. The Scandinavians erected crosses over the graves of their kings long before the Christians used them for a similar purpose. The cross was a symbol of life to the ancient Egyptians and was a sacred symbol to the Aztecs before they had any contact with the Christians' symbol.

The crucifixion of Jesus provided a focal point for the grafting on to the Christian religion of a symbol which was already held in veneration by many of the earth's peoples. It is significant that the first specifically Christian symbol was not the cross at all, but the *Ichthus* or fish, because the word is formed of the initial letters of *Jesous Christos, Theou Uios Soter* (Jesus Christ, Son of God, Saviour). This was used as a sign of recognition among the brethren when Christianity was a secret society, banned by the state, in Rome.

The cross used for crucifixion was normally the 'tau cross', shaped like the letter T, so that it cannot be truly said to provide the basis for the symbol of Christianity. It was the identification of Christ with one of the members of the Trinity of Godhead which gave the main impetus to its use; Christ was, to the Christians, God-made-material, hence the 'Son of Man'. The cross as a symbol relates to the *materiality* of Jesus in its original connotations, whatever the later interpretations, for the cross is the one symbol which is of the earth entirely.

An interesting sidelight on the identification of the four cardinal points with created man is the possible Greek derivation of the name Adam. It may or may not be coincidence that the four Greek letters which make up the name are the initial letters of the Greek words for East and West, North and South, i.e. *Anatole, Dusis, Arktos* and *Mesembria.*

In whatever form it appears, the number four relates to the material or earthly plane as opposed to the number three, which refers to the divine or spiritual. Plato said that the number three pertained to the Idea while the number four related to the *realisation* of the Idea. This is the same as the pattern of the Genesis creation story. The first three days are devoted to ordering the 'fields of potentiality' in which life can be generated. The forms of life are concretised in the next four days, of which the last, on which God rested, is the 'odd man out' mentioned in the quotation from C. G. Jung. There is a profound philosophical meaning to this last of the four days of 'giving life to the earth'. Right from the beginning of the creation story, it is stressed that the process of creation is one of separating the opposites; light is separated from darkness, heaven from earth, land from sea and so on. In the same way, the creation of active life is a separation of life from its reverse, death, and of activity from its reverse, rest. In this sense, the resting of God is a *creative* activity. This rest is, in the deepest sense, different from the state of equilibrium which precedes creation. This rest is a positive absence of activity in the same way that darkness is the absence of light. In the equilibrium of pre-creation, light and darkness are absorbed in each other, as are activity and rest. To borrow from the Hindus again, 'in Brahman, there is neither being nor non-being'.

This brings us into the sphere of Pythagorean number-philosophy:

One represents God-in-Himself, the ultimate First Cause, in which all things, all ideas and all opposites are reconciled.

Two represents duality, the inevitable polarity of creation. Since the state it represents is considered as a 'fall' from perfection, the number is conceived of as evil. In the masculine world in which Pythagoras lived, the God in Whom all polarity was extinguished still managed to be male in character; so One and all odd numbers were masculine, while Two and all even numbers were feminine.

Three represents God immanent in His creation because it has a beginning, a middle and an end. Related to the human plane, it represents the marriage of man (One) and woman (Two), creating a new life (Three). Geometrically, One is a point, hence the Centre of all; Two is seen as a line, that which joins two points, and therefore represents marriage; Three is the simplest plane figure possessing area or extension, the triangle, and so it represents the essence of creation which extends potentiality into space and time.

Four is Two times Two, the first square. It is therefore an intensification of the separative qualities of Two and represents gross materiality.

The Christian Tetramorphs, the symbols of the four Evangelists, have found expression in a great deal of Christian religious art. These symbols, the lion, eagle, ox and man (or angel), have their origins in remotest antiquity. A Sumerian relief shows a lion, an eagle and a peacock standing on the back of an ox. In the Old Testament, Ezekiel has a vision containing the lion, eagle, ox and man.

It is fairly obvious that the symbolism of the Tetramorphs, like that of the earlier versions, is similar in essence to that of the four Elements, earth, air, fire and water. All material things may be described as varying combinations of these Elements:

Earth — the idea of solidity, weight, resistance,
Water — fluidity, conformation, passivity,
Air — space, freedom of movement, expansion,
Fire — basic energy, force, thrust.

It will be noticed that each of these Elements can be considered as one of a pair of opposites. Fire and water are opposed, for either one can eliminate the other; air and earth are opposed, the one being fixed, resistant, immovable and the other free flowing, full of the potential for

movement. This is in line with the idea of the polarisations of creation.

The attributes of the Tetramorphs, or the four symbolic animals, may be used in the same way:

The Lion is all strength and fire,
The Eagle is free-roaming in the air,
The Ox is stolid, unmoving, resistant,
The Peacock is flowing, changeable.

So the lion is the equivalent of fire, the eagle of air, the ox of earth and the peacock of water. The Christian Tetramorphs substitute the man for the peacock. If we retain the symbolism, we have to admit that we find a rather cynical view of man as conforming, easily-influenced, unpredictable, etc.

Leaving such considerations aside and returning to our main theme of the significance of the number four, there can be no doubt that, from the earliest times, this number has always referred to the material, usually to matter directly, but when it is related to man, it signifies the mortal who lives here on earth, eating, loving and sleeping, rather than man as a spiritual entity.

The Centre

The symbol of the mystic Centre is common to all forms of religious expression which stress individual mystical experience more than the dogmas of revelation.

This Centre is equivalent to the 'unmoved mover' of Aristotle. It is the seat of the ultimate Creator, ever at rest yet ever active. In man, it is the 'observer', intimately connected with man's experiences and actions but itself outside of them. Because we believe this concept to be one which is essential to the symbolism of the sacred number, we propose to examine it in some detail.

A good starting point is the theory of relativity as it stands at the moment, for the most outstanding feature of modern mathematical physics is the role played by the *observer* in the results obtained from experiments. It was from a single axiom that the whole of the Special Theory of Relativity was built. This axiom states that, for *any* observer, the speed of light from any source, moving or not relative to the observer, is always the same.

At first glance, this does not seem a very startling assumption but if we examine it carefully, we find that it leads to a paradox which cannot be resolved by our minds, conditioned as they are to judging everything from a mechanical standpoint.

Imagine that we are travelling towards a distant planet at a speed of 200,000 km per second. On the planet stands a man with a flashlight which he shines towards us. He measures the speed of the light-ray leaving his torch and finds it to be 300,000 km per second. What result do we expect to get when we measure this same ray of light as it reaches us? Surely, we must add our own speed towards the light to that of the light towards us and we should then expect our instruments to record a total speed of 500,000 km per second. But no! We shall find, in fact, that the light is being received by us at exactly the same

THE QUATERNARY

speed at which it left the planet towards which we are travelling, 300,000 km per second. If we used our measurement of the incoming light to try to determine how fast we were travelling towards it, we should have to conclude that we were standing still!

We have referred to this unchangeability of the *measured* speed of light as an axiom, but it should be mentioned that many experiments have been carried out to test its validity and the results have always confirmed it completely. The philosophical implication is that the observer himself is the 'cause' of the constant speed of all light reaching him.

A similarly paradoxical result is produced when we assess the experimental results connected with the production of interference patterns on a fluorescent screen by streams of photons from a single source directed towards the screen through a pair of holes in an otherwise opaque plate. The fact that a single photon (a 'quantum' of light) can be made to produce a point of scintillation on the screen constrains the experimenter to treat light as if it were a stream of particles. If he does so, however, he is faced with the 'impossible' result that each photon passes through both holes simultaneously before reaching the screen. The scientist does not try to force such a mechanistic interpretation upon us, however. Instead, he stresses the impossibility of ever determining how a single photon travels in such an experiment *because the action of observing the photon interferes with, and helps to determine, its flight*. Again he is saying that the results of the experiment depend on the observer.

Psychoanalysts who make use of the dreams of their patients know that they can never become aware of the 'normal' dream-states of the people with whom they deal. As soon as the therapy gets under way, the patient begins to report the kind of dreams the therapist expects, even if he has apparently never produced such dreams before. The act of observing them is the 'cause' of the dreams and so the analyst is, to some extent, getting back what his observations have projected into the patient.

Something similar happens in introspection. When we are sitting daydreaming, our phantasies tumble over each other, being realised in rapid succession, but as soon as we make a decision to observe their arrival and departure, they simply cease to flow. The deliberate act of observation appears to stifle their activity completely.

The modern scientific view of individual consciousness therefore supports the view that it is not just a sort of mental cinema screen which passively allows events to be projected upon itself. On the contrary, it appears to be an active participant in whatever it observes. One is tempted to take this idea to its logical conclusion and say that the observer *creates* the objects of his observations. Perhaps man *is* created in the image of God; perhaps he is the microcosmic creator, a reflection of God, the macrocosmic Creator.

Whatever the relationship implied by this supposition, we cannot help seeing ourselves individually as a centre — *the* centre — of awareness around which the objects of consciousness seem to orbit like planets around the sun. In Hindu philosophy, as we have already noted, this Centre, which is the innermost essence of man, stripped of all outside objects and images, is identical with the Supreme Creator. The Atman is one with the Brahman.

This notion of identity is not confined to a single religious system. It constitutes the background to, and the aim of, all mystical activity, with whatever particular religious trappings it is clothed.

'I and the Father are One. Whoever has seen Me has seen the Father.'

We feel intuitively that whatever is at the centre of a system is the most important part of the system. The sun is the leader of our local cosmic hierarchy not simply because it is the brightest object in the sky but mainly because the other members of the system revolve around it. In Egyptian hieroglyphics, the sun is represented not by a simple disc, as one might expect, but by a circle with a dot in the centre, symbolising its *central* character. Following the symbolism of the ternary and quaternary, the pyramid sun-symbol tells the story of creation in stone. It starts with the apex — or centre — from which creation emanates; the triangular sides denote the process of creation as the realisation of the three principles, while the square base refers to the concrete results of creation. It can be seen how apt a symbol the pyramid is in this connection. The square at its base is coincident with the earth which it represents, while the triangles of creative principles spread out from the apex like the rays of the sun. It is obvious that, for the pyramid-builders, the Creator *was* the sun or, at least, that the sun was His visible symbol.

From the point of view of our investigation, we see already in the pyramid-building age that the combined triangle and square, which represents the number Seven, had a well-developed sacred background and that the idea of the Centre as Creator is implicit in the pyramid, the solid symbol of the sacred number.

4
In The Beginning...

We have seen that the number seven, or three plus four, is the number of creation. The ternary represents the divine principles through which the act of creation is accomplished, while the quaternary represents the created universe and the elements of which it is composed. The way in which the three principles generate the four elements is analogous to the way in which the three primary colours generate the four 'mixture' colours and this analogy explains the 'odd man out' among the elements of the quaternary, one element being of a different character from the other three. The odd colour-mixture is brown, the only colour containing all three of the primary colours. In the traditional elements, fire is the odd one because it is a transmutation whereas the other three are substances.

Philosophically, this is all quite sound, but we want to get behind philosophy to find out what was the trigger which set humanity thinking along the lines which produced this particular pattern of ideas as a culmination. Symbols, which have different levels of meaning, each appealing to the human mind at a different level of evolution, *preceded* philosophy and had their effects on man's instinctive reactions and on his emotions before he learned to think about them rationally, to realise them intuitively or to know them through his spiritual essence.

The creation myths of mankind are invariably his most ancient traditions and can provide us with an insight into the kind of thoughts and reactions which occupied man's mind at the time when the creation-number was becoming fixed as something sacred.

Now we find when we examine them that the creation myths of mankind all over the world are remarkably similar.* They fall into two categories, the details of which are often transferred from one to the

*See Appendix 1.

other as though, over the thousands of years in which they have been repeated orally, the two basic stories have become confused. The first category is the 'philosophical' story of the creation of the world out of the primeval Void, such as the seven-day creation story of Genesis. We call such a story 'philosophical' because it is bound to be pure conjecture, since, by its very nature, true creation can have no witness 'in the beginning'. The second category is really quite different; it refers to the *re-creation* of man after the destruction of the world by some great catastrophe, usually fire followed by flood. This second category, represented in the Bible by the stories of Noah and Lot, is by far the more common and its basic elements are almost invariable. The god or gods see that mankind is sinful and decide to destroy the earth. First, fire is rained down from heaven upon the earth and destroys all living things except those which have sheltered in a cave or have found some similar means of escape. Then a great flood covers the earth and drowns all except those who have been warned and escape in a boat or ark and who then become the progenitors of the new human race.

There are few peoples or tribes, from the Polynesians of the South Pacific to the Norsemen of the frozen North, who do not have either a tradition of the destruction of the earth by fire or by flood – or both. For this reason, we should be irrational if we did not accept that these myths *represent a race-memory of an actual catastrophe* of such tremendous proportions that it affected the whole earth; but let us first look at some of the actual stories which have come down to us in writing and by word of mouth so that we can form a balanced judgement.

The Philosophical Creation-myths
The Phoenician creation story was attributed by Philo Byblos (A.D. 42 to 117) to Sanchuniathon (11th Century B.C.). It tells how, in the beginning, there existed Air and Chaos, who produced Wind and Desire, from whom came Mot, the primeval egg, out of which came the heavenly bodies, the sun, moon and stars. Later, the symbolic parents Genos and Genea (the male and female principles) begat three children, Light, Fire and Flame. To Light fell the duty of creating order by separating the waters from the sky.

In the Chinese creation myth, Chaos divided itself into the male and female principles, Yin and Yang, from whom came the giant whose body composed the universe.

IN THE BEGINNING...

These two stories are typical of the *genre* we are discussing. The pre-existent being or state is either chaos or an earth-mother goddess. If the former, the first act of creation is one of polarisation and this is followed by the production of a triad who create the world; if the latter, she either begets the other two members of the triad and remains part of it herself or she produces three children who become the creative triad. Such stories are the result of applying philosophical thought to the world picture created by the particular tribal environment or way of life. They all have the flavour of 'this is the way it must have been'.

The Fire and Deluge Myths

Strictly speaking, these stories should not be called creation myths at all. The reason they are grouped with the true creation myths is that the latter often contain features suggesting an overlap of ideas from the former. Thus in the Genesis creation story, the primeval state implied by literal interpretation is one in which there is only water, which is then separated by God into the waters above and below the firmament and again the lower waters are separated from the land. We can see clearly in these images the emergence of the world from the flood, although the Deluge proper is the subject of a later, and quite different, story in which Noah figures.

The triad mentioned in the Creation tablets which came from the library of Ashurbanipal (c. 650 B.C.) contain a similar overlap of ideas. The triad consists of Apsu, Mommu and Tiamat and they are said to have existed from the beginning of time. From them sprang all the gods and demons. But Apsu represents sweet water; Tiamat is the god of bitter water and Mommu is a sort of intermediary between them. However, the examples which follow are all catastrophe myths.

A Bolivian myth tells how a great conflagration was followed by a flood. The earth's inhabitants sheltered in a great cave. The entrance to the cave became blocked, making it extremely difficult to get out and the only living creatures which emerged were monkeys. The world was, however, repopulated by a triad, Titl, Ule and his wife.

A Guianan story tells how Sigu decided to cut down the Tree of Knowledge in order to plant its seeds all over the earth. Water gushed from the stump and flooded the earth. Sigu led the humans into a cave for safety.

According to Aztec myth, the earth was destroyed by floods caused by the water-sun (Atonaitiuh), after which the wind-sun caused earthquakes.

Berossus (c. 280 B.C.) tells of the Babylonian tradition that the original abyss of waters was ruled by the goddess Thalath, whose name signifies the sea or the moon. She was cut in two by Belus, the two halves forming heaven and earth. Xisuthros was warned of a coming flood and was told to build a ship after burying the records of the past, and thus he survived the flood.

The Cashinava Indians of West Brazil say that torrential rains drowned every living thing. This was followed by the heavens bursting and huge rocks falling upon the earth.

The Cato Indians of California, in common with many other North American Indian tribes, say that the world was set on fire and blazed until the thunder god sent great rains which drowned most of the world.

In the Celtic myths of Ireland, Bith and his wife, Birren, together with their family escaped the flood by ship to Innisfail. Later, they were all killed when a large red moon with bright expanding clouds broke up into hundreds of pieces, which fell upon the earth.

In China, the myth of Kung-Kung relates that he butted down the pillars of heaven, causing the firmament to collapse and the waters above it to fall on the earth and flood it.

Even the ancient Egyptians had a flood myth. They said that the flood was caused by Atmu, the primeval god, and that only those who were in a boat with him escaped. In the waters was Nun, the chaos monster. The sun then rose from the waters and divided them from the sky. Four pillars were erected at the cardinal points to hold up the sky.

The Iroquois Indians have a curious story that Athensic, the ancestress of the human race, fell from the sky into the waters as the floods were receding. When the land dried out where she was, it became a great continent. Compare this with the story told by the Muyscaya Indians, who attribute the flood to the goddess Chia. As the earth was then without a moon, she was turned into the present moon by way of punishment.

In Nordic legend, the flood was caused by the blood of Imir the giant when he was killed by the four sons of Bor. It was from Imir's body that the world had originally been created.

A Brazilian myth-complex, which mentions both fire and flood, has the moon as the power of evil because it periodically falls upon the earth and destroys it.

IN THE BEGINNING ...

The Common Elements of the Catastrophe Myths

Stories similar to the examples quoted above are told by nations and tribes in every part of the world and similar elements are contained in almost all of them. The moon, or a moon-god or goddess, is one such common element. This would be understandable if floods alone were attributed to the moon's influence, since a flood can be likened to a specially high tide, but we often find the *fire-catastrophe* being connected with the moon's influence in the same way. The most graphic description in this connection is the large, red moon with bright expanding clouds, mentioned in the Celtic myth. The Washo Indian tribe reverse the causes and effects by saying that the fires on the earth melted the stars, which then fell on to the earth. There is a similar reversal between the stories of Athensic falling to earth, on the one hand, and Chia being made into the moon on the other hand. In the Babylonian story, the moon was cut in two, while in a variant of the Egyptian myth previously quoted, Ra orders two goddesses to destroy the earth by fire, the goddesses being Sekhmet and Hathor. Now Sekhmet was known as the goddess of fire, so her part in the affair is easy to understand, but *Hathor was the cow-headed moon-goddess*.

There are far more catastrophe-legends which mention floods than fire, but where fire is not mentioned, rocks falling from the sky are often a feature of the stories. Often, humanity is said to shelter from the flood in a cave. It is obvious that a cave gives no protection from flood waters, but it is a most effective shelter from the effects of fire and falling rocks and it need occasion no surprise that caves are usually prominent in the fire myths. We can assume with some certainty that, where caves are mentioned, a fire or rock-falling catastrophe is implied even when there is no other reference to it. In the course of many thousands of word-of-mouth repetitions, mutilations and omissions would be cumulative and whole sections of the original stories could be completely forgotten. For many peoples, in any case, fire is reckoned as man's greatest discovery, his benevolent protector from the cold and the medium of his food preparation. Such peoples would find it extremely difficult to equate fire with world-wide disaster.

The Race Memory Implied by the Myths

Anyone who spends some time examining and comparing the hundreds of catastrophe-creation myths of the world is forced, by their similarity, to conclude that all point to an actual event which occurred at some period when man was beginning to develop settled communities.

There is no doubt that the catastrophe was connected with the moon, that it involved something falling from the heavens and that it caused widespread fires and floods on an unprecedented scale, which destroyed a large part of humanity and of the flora and fauna of the earth. Since the fire, rock-falls, earthquakes and floods are almost invariably part of the same story, they must all have been due to a single cause.

Now, what could cause all these effects on a scale which affected the whole world in one way or another? The moon, as is suggested by many of the stories? No, for she still rides there serenely in the sky. What we have to look for is *another* moon. Gurdjieff, who spent some years listening to the legends of the Russians, Chinese, Indians and other peoples, claimed to have discovered definite indications that there was a time when the earth had a second moon.

Only one type of cosmic event can account for *all* the phenomena recounted in the myths. An asteroid, or similar body of considerable size, with a very eccentric orbit, came within the earth's gravitational field at such a speed and in such a direction as to be put into temporary orbit around the earth. Its new orbit would be a spiral which caused the body to come closer and closer to the earth over a period which might have been a year, a hundred years or even a thousand years, since we have no means of computing its orbit in retrospect. To the inhabitants of the earth, the new body would have the appearance and characteristics of a second moon, giving light at night and going through regular phases. Since we must presume it to have been very much less massive than the moon itself, its orbit round the earth and, therefore, its phases, would be very much more rapid than the moon's.

Until the spiral orbit brought the body fairly close to the earth, its gravitational effects would be quite small, but as it came lower, these would increase rapidly. Once it reached a certain point, the speed of 'fall' of the little moon would increase exponentially, so that the real catastrophe can be presumed to have taken effect in quite a short period, giving little warning that it was about to happen except to those skilled enough to read the signs correctly.

The first noticeable effect would be on the sea, with large tides being thrown up due to the object's gravity. These would not yet be of cataclysmic proportions but they would be enough to warn man that something bigger was coming. The second moon would, by this time, look huge in the sky and, with its rapidly changing phases and frequent

IN THE BEGINNING ... 59

eclipses, would be an awesome thing, but not as terrifying as the next phase of the catastrophe, which was that the interaction of the gravitational fields of the earth and its captured satellite tore the latter asunder into two pieces, one of which, on entering the outer regions of the atmosphere, exploded into a veritable hailstorm of huge rocks which fell, burning, towards the earth. These rocks were obviously large enough to reach the surface without burning up completely and their heat set fire to forests in widely-spread areas of the world. The larger section would now appear to have hit the earth in one piece in the middle of one of the oceans, probably the Atlantic, its impact causing a tidal wave large enough to encircle the earth, submerging whole islands as far away as the Pacific and flooding great areas of the continents. The impact started a chain-reaction causing new faults in the earth's crust in what is now recognised as the earthquake belt and bringing into being new volcanoes.

Imagine the effect of all these terrifying phenomena on the minds of those men who, for one reason or another, survived them! Their descriptions would be handed down from generation to generation, the awesome work of the gods being described in all its lurid detail, which needed no additions from the imagination for its effect.

The Development of the Number Symbol
To those who lived through the early part of the catastrophe, the preliminary signs in the heavens must have had immense significance. The number of the heavenly bodies involved was three: the sun, the 'good' moon and the 'evil' moon. As events developed, this heavenly triad caused *fire* to fall from heaven, *water* to well up from the deep, great rushing movements of the *air* and the buckling and crumbling of the *earth*. Are these not the four elements of creation? And are they not likely to be mentioned separately by every eye-witness to the cataclysm?

As memory faded and the story developed from pure account of fact into myth, the three heavenly bodies became transmuted into three gods or, philosophically, into three principles, while the earth, air, fire and water features, constantly repeated, fitted into poetic sagas and, adorned with more abstract qualities, became the elements used by the gods to re-create, and, eventually, to *create* the earth and its inhabitants. Separation of parts and the development of individual features are common processes in mythology, but in this case the development is really very slight; the three gods and the four elements have remained connected almost in the form in which they originated. The septenary in its three-plus-four pattern is thus seen to have a concrete historical basis on which the later philosophers were able to build and we have found a powerful reason for the numinous quality of the number seven.

5
Counting and the Practical Uses of Numbers

Nomadic man had little use for number. Even today, the languages of some undeveloped peoples contain names for only three numerical categories, 'one', 'two' and 'many'. In his communications with his fellow-men, the nomad has no need to specify exact numbers. If he wants to tell them there are animals worth hunting in the woods over there, it is not important to know whether there are five or twelve of them; it is sufficient that there are *some*.

It is only when man forms settled communities and begins to develop specialised occupations that he learns the art of trading, which is the incentive to name individual numbers. Community living is different from nomadic life in that the tribe becomes a functioning unit, with one section responsible for the hunting, one for guarding the women, one for making clothing, one for cultivating plant-food and so on. Inevitably, the following of specialised occupations leads to barter. If I make clothing and you grow maize, sooner or later, I shall want to trade one of my coats for so many of your ears of corn and I shall want to argue with you about the number of ears you must give me. At first, perhaps, I shall be satisfied to accept a pile 'about so high', but quite soon I shall see that there is a difference between the number being offered by you and by another man and shall have to have some means of communicating the difference to you.

Counting involves the naming of numbers only as a secondary development. Initially, all we need to do is to make tally marks in the sand or raise so many fingers to indicate the number we wish to communicate. This is a matter of what the mathematicians refer to as putting two sets into one-to-one correspondence with each other. Each tally mark corresponds to one of the objects being counted. Difficulty arises, however, when we want to compare two different numbers. We may make two sets of tally marks and, by inspection, decide that one is greater than the other, but this becomes progressively more difficult as the numbers get larger and, in any case, does not enable us to say what the difference between the two numbers is. We really need a *standard set* of numbers with which to compare them both.

The most readily available, completely portable and constantly reproduceable set of objects which can provide such a standard is the set of fingers on the hand. It is easy to 'tick off' one finger for each object being counted and we have a ready-made name for the number represented by all the fingers on one hand; we simply call it a 'hand'. If I say to you 'Give me a hand of ears of corn plus one ear', you can count out the required amount without difficulty.

Now we can combine this method with our tally marks in the sand to count off larger numbers. Since we have two hands, let us call the total of both sets of fingers a 'two-hand' and agree that, in counting, we shall make a tally mark every time we complete a two-hand. Similarly, when the number of tally marks is equal to the number of our fingers, we can erase the marks we have made and make one mark of a different shape. This mark will now represent a 'two-hand of two-hands', or, in modern language, one hundred. All that now remains is to make our counting system suitable for *remembering* the numbers. And so we give each of the numbers from one to a hand or from one to a two-hand a distinctive name. Now we can count verbally, thus: 'One, two, three, four, hand, hand-one, hand-two, hand-three, hand-four, two-hand, two-hand and one, two-hand and two. . . . ' and so on.

This is the origin of the base 10 of our system of enumeration and it shows itself clearly in the tally marks or figures used by ancient peoples.

The Mayas actually used 20 as the base of their system, but its derivation from the hand is obvious in the design of the numerals.

COUNTING AND THE PRACTICAL USES OF NUMBERS   63

Ancient Egyptian hieroglyphics have a numeral system based on the two-hand.

I	II	III III III	∩	∩∩	∩∩∩ ∩∩∩ ∩∩∩
1	2	9	10	20	90

Roman numerals, although more complicated in operation (e.g. four is shown as one before five) are based on the hand – V – and the two-hand – a V the right way up joined to a V upside down, making X, thus:

I	II	III	IV	V
1	2	3	4	5

VI	VII	VIII	IX	X
6	7	8	9	10

The Attic system of counting, used in Greece in the 6th Century BC, was also a decimal system, but with a sub-base of 5. The figures themselves were based on the initial letters of the names of the units:

The Penta sign was combined with the signs for multiples of 10 as follows:

$$50 - \boxed{\Delta}$$
$$500 - \boxed{H}$$
$$5000 - \boxed{X}$$
$$50000 - \boxed{M}$$

The number 6789 would thus be written as:

The ancient Chinese used a system of horizontal and vertical bars in which the hundreds signs repeated the units signs, the thousands signs repeated the tens signs and so on up the scale of increasing powers of 10:

1 or 100	∣	10 or 1000	—
3 or 300	∣∣∣	20 or 2000	═
5 or 500	∣∣∣∣∣	50 or 5000	≡
6 or 600	⊤	70 or 7000	⊥
9 or 900	∣∣∣∣	80 or 8000	⫴

Such systems were completely adequate to deal with the counting problems of the market place in spite of certain drawbacks to which we shall refer later. Their adequacy is shown by the fact that, with one modification, we still use the decimal system to this day. The modification, though small in itself, is of immense practical importance. It is

COUNTING AND THE PRACTICAL USES OF NUMBERS

the use of *place values*. In the old systems shown above, each new power of 10 had to be given a new name and a new type of tally mark to distinguish it from the lower orders. This involved a multiplication of symbols which taxed both the ingenuity of the originators and the memory of the scribes. By contrast, we use only ten symbols to represent any number we like, the position in the number determining the power of 10 by which each figure must be multiplied. Thus there is a units position, a tens position, a hundreds position and so on. Such position-writing is made possible by the use of the symbol 0 to mark those positions which are *empty* in the number.

The Arab mathematicians of the Middle Ages are usually credited with the invention of a symbol to represent zero, but the position-writing principle was already known and used (albeit inconsistently) by the ancient Babylonians nearly 4000 years ago. There are extant cuneiform tablets from this era in which position-writing of numbers is used extensively, with a small mark used between two figures to indicate an empty position. But, possibly because the Babylonian mathematicians were more concerned with *proportionate* quantities than with absolute values, they never used their zero mark at the *end* of a number. So, while a number analogous to 202 would be clearly rendered, the value of the number written as 22 could be 22, 220, 2200, 22000 etc., its order having to be determined from the context in which it occurred.

Symbolic Significance Related to Practical Use
Two numbers stand out as significant in this development of counting systems; they are 5, the 'hand', and 10, the 'two-hand'. As we have shown, 10 was equivalent to 1, but in a higher order, so its symbolic significance for the ancients, if it acquired any, would be based entirely upon that of unity. There is, however, in the relationship between 5 and 10 a possible reinforcement of the mystical significance of the number 7, for 10 is equal to 5 times 2 and has no other factors. But if we *add* 5 and 2, we get the magic number, 7. Again, 5 multiplied by itself is 25 and 2 plus 5 is 7, while 2 multiplied by itself is 4, the quaternary component of 7. If we subtract 7 from 10, we get 3, the ternary component of 7.

Such computations may seem trivial and arbitrary as, from a mathematical standpoint, they are, but they are no more so than the computations used by modern numerologists to prove, for instance, that the number derived from the name Adolph Hitler signifies 'evil multiplied by itself'. Nor are they any less significant than the complicated system of biblical interpretation based on numbers developed by the Cabalists.

All we are looking for here is evidence of the psychological reinforcement of the significance attached to a particular number and, if the computations mentioned are seen as significant by the people who make them, the reinforcement will be automatic.

In connection with this particular relationship, we can find an example in the Genesis story of creation, where the expression 'God said' is used 10 times, while 'God saw' is used 7 times, 'God made' is used 4 times and 'God blessed' and also 'God called' are used 3 times. In view of the emphasis in Genesis on the number 7, it cannot be coincidence that the numbers 10, 7, 4 and 3 are used together in these circumstances. The intention must have been to draw attention to the relationship between them.

The Tetractys

The Pythagoreans had a symbol which was venerated by them, called the tetractys. Based on the number 10, this figure demonstrates the relationships between the numbers we have been discussing. The tetractys, shown below, is a visual demonstration of a fact which appeared highly significant to the Pythagoreans, namely that 1 plus 2 plus 3 plus 4 is 10.

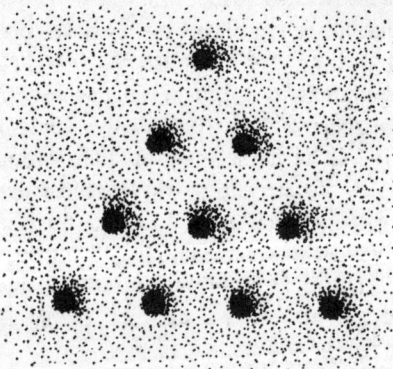

Mathematically, 10 is just one of an infinite series of numbers called the triangular numbers, formed by adding together successive integers, starting with 1. Thus, 1 2 3 4 5 and 6, when added together, make 21,

COUNTING AND THE PRACTICAL USES OF NUMBERS 67

so 21 is a triangular number and, like 10, can be arranged in the form of a triangle. The first ten triangular numbers are 1, 3, 6, 10, 15, 21, 28, 36, 45 and 55.

The square numbers are formed in a similar way, starting with 1 and adding successive *odd* numbers.

Add 1 and 3 and you get 4, which is the square of 2
1, 3 and 5 gives 9, which is the square of 3
1, 3, 5 and 7 gives 16, which is the square of 4
1, 3, 5, 7 and 9 gives 25, which is the square of 5, etc.

Just as the triangular numbers are capable of being represented by dots arranged in a triangular formation, the square numbers can be arranged in squares as shown below:

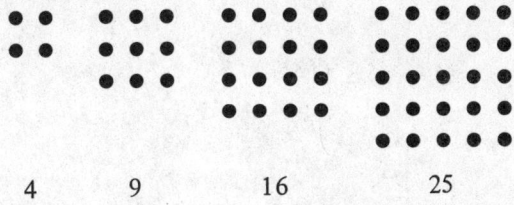

    4   9   16   25

As a matter of interest, if the square numbers are added together, starting with 1, the results are pyramidal numbers, which can be arranged in three dimensions in the form of a pyramid, in which successive layers are the square numbers. Each 'face' of the pyramid will be a triangular number.

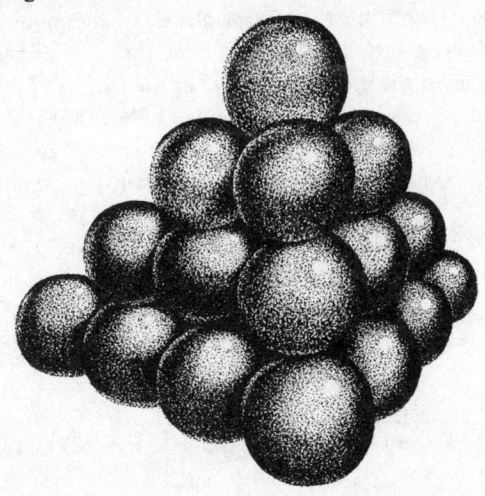

To return to the tetractys, the Pythagorean interpretation of the figure is that the apex represents One, the First Cause, while the second row is Two, signifying polarity. The first two rows together are Three, the Trinity of creation, and this is the first, and simplest, triangle. But Three is reflected in the third row, while the fourth row is Four, the first square number. Any number from 1 to 10 can be made up by adding two or more rows together, but there is special significance in the fact that any line drawn through the figure so that it is separated into two sets of two rows has on one side of it the Trinity and on the other the Septenary with its components, the Ternary and Quaternary. If the three points of the triangle are removed, this elegantly symmetrical figure remains, the septenary in its 'planetary' aspect:

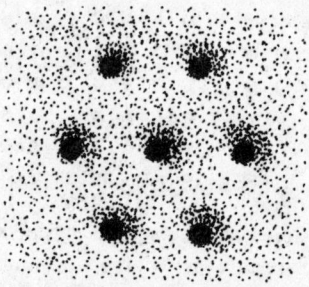

An interesting feature of the triangular number series is that the *seventh* in the series is 28, which is itself 4 times 7. This number is the number of days taken by the visible phases of the moon. It is also a 'perfect' number, a rare breed of numbers, the total of the factors of which are equal to the number itself. Thus the factors of 28 are 1, 2, 4, 7 and 14 and if these are added together, the result is 28. Only five perfect numbers occur in the first billion numbers. They are 6, 28, 496, 8128 and 33,550,336. *Now these are also triangular numbers.* 6 is the third triangular number, 28 is the 7th, 496 the 31st, 8128 the 127th and 33,550,336 the 8191st. It remains to be proved that *all* perfect numbers are necessarily triangular in form, but the proof is beyond the scope of this book and beyond the mathematical ability of the present writer.*

---

*Since writing this, I find that there is a quite simple proof given by W. J. Reichmann in *The Fascination of Numbers* (Methuen and Co. Ltd, 1957).

COUNTING AND THE PRACTICAL USES OF NUMBERS

The Antedeluvian King-lists

Both the Babylonians and the Hebrews had traditions concerning the kings or patriarchs who ruled before the flood. Various Babylonian lists are known, in which the names of the kings vary, but their number is invariably ten. In Genesis, the number of patriarchs listed from Adam to Noah is also ten. The biblical list gives the age of each patriarch when he begat his successor, then the number of years he lived afterwards and finally his age at death. The complete list is given in the following table:

	PATRIARCH	AGE WHEN SUCCESSOR BORN	YEARS AFTER SUCCESSOR BORN	AGE AT DEATH
1.	Adam	130	800	930
2.	Seth	105	807	912
3.	Enosh	90	815	905
4.	Kenan	70	840	910
5.	Mahalalel	65	830	895
6.	Jared	162	800	962
7.	Enoch	65	300	365
8.	Methuselah	187	782	969
9.	Lamech	182	595	777
10.	Noah	600*	350*	950
	Total	1656	6919	8575

*Before and after flood.

A cursory glance at these figures will show that they are not intended to represent actual ages and therefore the numbers must themselves be intended to convey some other information.* The first thing we notice is that there is always a common factor in the figures given in the first and second columns for each patriarch. If this proves nothing else, it shows that the figures are symbolic.

The text of the passage containing this list repeats exactly the same words for each of the patriarchs in describing their ages except in the case of the *seventh* patriarch, Enoch. All the others are said to die but,

*See Appendix Two.

'having walked with God, Enoch was seen no more, because God had taken him away.' It is also peculiar that, while the ages of the other patriarchs at death are all in the range between 750 and 1000 years, the age of Enoch when he was taken away is given as 365, the number of days in the year.

The ages of the first, second, fifth and seventh patriarchs when their successors were born were 130, 105, 65 and 65 respectively. These four numbers total 365. If we take the figures in the second column for the same four patriarchs, we find 800, 807, 830 and 300, which total 2737. The figures in the third column for the first three of them are 930, 912 and 895, the total of which is again 2737. This figure is 365 times 7 plus 182, the figure in the first column for the ninth patriarch and itself equal to 26 times 7, or half a year in days. The ninth patriarch has the obviously contrived figure of 777 in the third column, a figure which is reminiscent of the number of the Beast given in Revelation, 666. In the symbolism of numbers, 6 is 'deficient' and tripling it is stressing it to the utmost, so 666 signifies the ultimate evil. 777, on the other hand, stresses the creative idea of completion carried by the number 7 and we are led to the idea that the 'first dispensation', (i.e. the world before the flood) was complete with the ninth patriarch, a new dispensation being started by the tenth patriarch, Noah. If the figures are taken in a historical sense, it will be seen that the death of Lamech is put at five years before the flood. By contrast, the eighth patriarch, Methuselah, is presumed to have perished in the flood, which is why the figures in column one for the last three patriarchs total 969, the age of Methuselah at death.

The supposed lifetimes of all ten patriarchs are plotted on the chart (p. 71) from which we can see that, if the figures are taken to represent actual historical ages, Adam was still alive when the ninth patriarch was born!

That the figures given in this list are intended to have meaning in themselves is almost certain and it would seem in the highest degree probable that this meaning relates to time sequences just as the surface historical meaning does. We have already seen that the numbers 365 (days of the year), 7 (days of the week) and 26 (weeks of the half-year) feature in the list and we should therefore expect to see the number 12 (months of the year) equally well represented. The only obvious use of this number occurs in the row of figures relating to Kenan. The figure 70 in the first column is the expected lifespan of man (the biblical three-score and ten) in years. This is multiplied by 12 to give the figure

COUNTING AND THE PRACTICAL USES OF NUMBERS

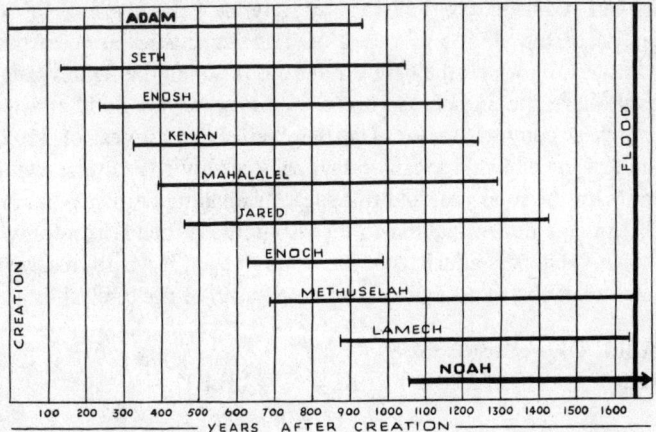

in the second column, 840, which is thus the expected lifetime of a man in months.

The total of the ages of all the patriarchs has the factor 7 three times ($8\,575 = 7^3$ times 5^2), while the number itself reduces to 7 by the process well-known to numerologists of adding the individual figures until a single figure results. Adding 8, 5, 7 and 5 gives 25 and adding 2 and 5 gives 7.

We turn now to the Babylonian lists of antedeluvian kings which was probably the prototype of the biblical list, to see whether it casts any light on the subject. The following is the list as given by Berossus:

	KING	REIGN IN YEARS	EXPRESSED TO BASE 60
1.	Alaros	36,000	10,0,0
2.	Alaparos	10,800	3,0,0
3.	Amelon	46,800	13,0,0
4.	Ammenon	43,200	12,0,0
5.	Megalaros	64,800	18,0,0
6.	Daonos	36,000	10,0,0
7.	Evedoraches	64,800	18,0,0
8.	Amempainos	36,000	10,0,0
9.	Opartes	28,800	8,0,0
10.	Xisuthros	64,800	18,0,0
	Total	432,000	2, 0,0,0

As can immediately be seen by reference to the list of years expressed in the counting system used for scientific purposes by the Babylonians, of which the base is not 10 but 60, all the figures given by Berossus have a common factor of 60 times 60, i.e. 3600 and this is their highest common factor. The Babylonians had a year of 360 days to which were added intercalary days as necessary to keep the civil year in step with the solar year and this suggests dividing Berossus' figures by 360, a process not unfamiliar to the Babylonians themselves, for whom one *divine* year was equal to 360 ordinary years. If we do this, we find we have a list comparable with the first column of the biblical list.

NUMBER OF RULER	BEROSSUS (DIVINE YEARS)	BIBLE
1	100	130
2	30	105
3	130	90
4	120	70
5	180	65
6	100	162
7	180	65
8	100	187
9	80	182
10	180	600
Total	1200	1656

Berossus' list is by no means the oldest list of antedeluvian kings. At least a millenium earlier, the Sumerians inscribed such a list on a tablet. Not unnaturally, the names given to the kings were different, but their number even then was ten. The following years, in 60-base figures, were allocated to them. (*See list on page 73.*)

It will be noticed at once that the first figure in this list is the only one which is not a round number and this makes it highly suspect. In cuneiform characters, this figure was written simply as 18,40, for, even at a late stage, the makers of cuneiform tablets did not insert a mark to represent zero at the end of a number. Also, no distinction was made between fractions of 60 and powers, so that the 40-part of this number could just as easily represent 40/60, i.e. 2/3. Suppose, then, that the scribe realised that he had made a mistake after writing 18 and wanted

COUNTING AND THE PRACTICAL USES OF NUMBERS

KING NUMBER	REIGN IN YEARS
1	18,40,0
2	20, 0,0
3	20, 0,0
4	6, 0,0
5	8, 0,0
6	6, 0,0
7	10, 0,0
8	20, 0,0
9	8, 0,0
10	10, 0,0
Total	2, 6,40,0

to correct this to read 12. One way would be to write 2/3 after the number, meaning 'take two thirds of it'. If we read this figure as 12,0,0 instead of 18,40,0, we find the total now agrees exactly with the total of Berossus' list, i.e. 2,0,0,0 years, or 1200 divine years.

This total, being the supposed length of time covered by the period from the creation to the flood, is naturally expected to be significant. In the Indian Mahabharata of about 400 BC, a Yuga, or world-age, consists of 1200 divine years and this suggests a common origin with the Babylonian king-lists. Is there a possible connection with the total of the biblical list? It has been suggested* that a connection can be traced through the idea of the Great (or Platonic) Year.

The ancients were aware of the phenomenon we now refer to as the precession of the equinoxes, the slow but continuous movement of the point in the heavens to which the poles of the earth's axis are directed. This point moves in a circle, the annual shift being 50.26 seconds of arc and it was measured with considerable accuracy by the ancient astronomers. The time taken by the poles to complete one circle in the heavens is the Great Year. We know that it was calculated that the movement becomes one degree of arc in 72 years, so a Great Year was reckoned as 360 times 72 years. The ancient Mesopotamians would certainly have been impressed by the fact that these two figures were the number of days in their year and the number of their five-day weeks in the same period. As we have already seen, it was not

*The Masks of God (Vol 2), Oriental Mythology, by Joseph Campbell

uncommon practice to use the numerical values connected with one time unit together with a different time unit, to produce, for instance, a week of years, a process which occurs several times in the Bible. Now if we divide the 1656 years of the biblical list by the 72 years required for the precession of one degree, the result is 23. Call these 23 'degree-years'. But 23 years consists of 8400 days, including the five leap-year days in the period and if we divide this figure by 7 to give the number of Hebrew weeks of seven days, we get the 1200 which is the total of the Babylonian lists.

Such a calculation sounds far-fetched to our modern ears, but it was in just such 'mysteries' that the ancient astronomer-priests wrapped their calculations, probably to make them less accessible to the common man, thereby increasing their own authority. The nomadic Hebrews did not have the astronomical skills of the Babylonians, but they did have a priesthood to whom many 'secrets' were entrusted. No doubt the Hebrew priests obtained copies of the Babylonian figures and, with their own love of number-symbolism, adapted them to their own different culture. The Babylonians had developed calculation to a high degree and were well versed in astronomical observation and computation. To the Hebrews, on the other hand, the main use of figures in the practical sense was for trading purposes.

We have already noticed that the idea of a world-age of so many divine years was common to the Babylonians and the Hindus, the figure they derived being 1200 divine years, which is equal to 432,000 ordinary years. Rather surprisingly, this figure crops up in similar connections in other cultures. In the Icelandic Poetic Edda, for instance, the following lines occur:

> *Five hundred doors and forty there are,*
> *I ween, in Valhall's walls;*
> *Eight hundred fighters through each door fare*
> *When to war with the Wolf they go.*

Since the 'war with the Wolf' refers to the battle marking the end of a cosmic age, the total number of fighters (years?) represented by this verse, i.e. 540 times 800 or 432,000, is specially significant.

The Sexagesimal System

The figure 432,000 is much more simple than it looks. It is 60^3 times 2 and this fact gives us a clear lead to its origin. It is the number written as 2,0,0,0 in the sexagesimal system of numeration in which the base is

COUNTING AND THE PRACTICAL USES OF NUMBERS

60. If we used this system nowadays, we should call this number 'two thousand' and we are reminded of the line in the well-known hymn which runs:

> *A thousand ages in Thy sight*
> *Are like an evening gone.*

No doubt a similar idea was in the minds of those who first used the number to represent a divine age.

However, as our concern is with the numbers themselves, this may be a good time to look into the origins of the use of the sexagesimal system by the ancient Babylonians.

Let us first note that they used *both* the sexagesimal and the decimal systems, the latter being the common mode for commercial and domestic reckoning while the former was used only for astronomical and scientific calculations.

We can be sure that the system originated as a direct result of its usefulness in astronomy. The ancient Chinese were also advanced in astronomical calculation and we know that they reckoned their days, months and years in cycles of 60 units, which arise in an interesting way. Two word-units are used by the Chinese to name their time units, a stem and a suffix, known as the 'celestial stem' and the 'terrestrial branch'. There are 10 celestial stems and 12 terrestrial branches and each is used in sequence until all possible combinations have been exhausted, when a new cycle begins. This gives 60 combinations as can be seen from the table.

1 Chia-Tzu	16 Chi-Mao	31 Chia-Wu	46 Chi-Yu
2 I-Ch'ou	17 Keng-Ch'en	32 I-Wei	47 Keng-Hsu
3 Ping-Ying	18 Hsin-Szu	33 Ping-Shen	48 Hsin-Hai
4 Ting-Mao	19 Jen-Wu	34 Ting-Yu	49 Jen-Tzu
5 Wu-Ch'en	20 Kuei-Wei	35 Wu-Hsu	50 Kuei-Ch'ou
6 Chi-Szu	21 Chia-Shen	36 Chi-Hai	51 Chia-Ying
7 Keng-Wu	22 I-Yu	37 Keng-Tzu	52 I-Mao
8 Hsin-Wei	23 Ping-Hsu	38 Hsin-Ch'ou	53 Ping-Ch'en
9 Jen-Shen	24 Ting-Hai	39 Jen-Ying	54 Ting-Szu
10 Kuei-Yu	25 Wu-Tzu	40 Kuei-Mao	55 Wu-Wu
11 Chia-Hsu	26 Chi-Ch'ou	41 Chia-Ch'en	56 Chi-Wei
12 I-Hai	27 Keng-Ying	42 I-Szu	57 Keng-Shen
13 Ping-Tzu	28 Hsin-Mao	43 Ping-Wu	58 Hsin-Yu
14 Ting-Ch'ou	29 Jen-Ch'en	44 Ting-Wei	59 Jen-Hsu
15 Wu-Ying	30 Kuei-Szu	45 Wu-Shen	60 Kuei-Hai

As the Chinese calendar is lunar, the use of the number 12, the completed number of lunations in a year, is natural, while the number 10 is the ordinary base of their counting system. It is a happy coincidence that the resulting number, 60, in days is almost exactly equal to two lunations and that 6 cycles of days is almost equal to the length of the solar year. The Chinese civil year actually consisted of 12 lunations of alternatively 30 days (big-month) and 29 days (little month) plus one intercalary month inserted every three years to adjust the civil to the solar year.

The Babylonians arrived at their sexagesimal system by a quite different route, although some of the same considerations doubtless settled its use. In the case of the Babylonians, its origin was primarily geometrical and it arose from two quite unconnected geometrical considerations, one being concerned with the measurement of the heavens and the other with the measurement of the earth. As we shall show, both are intimately connected with the sacred number seven and we shall therefore look at them in some detail.

The Idea of the Right Angle

We have discussed in the chapter dealing with the quaternary the considerations which necessitate the four directions of space as the minimum number by reference to which *any* direction can be specified without pointing.

There is, of course, no difficulty in visualising these four directions mentally, but to make an exact model of them in the form of a cross which can be laid out on the ground is not as easy as it might appear. This is the starting point for the study of the right angle and it became of increasing importance as man began to construct large buildings.

Columbia University, N.Y. possesses a clay tablet into which cuneiform characters were impressed 2000 years before Christ. Known as the Plimpton 322 tablet, it proves that, even at this remote time, the Babylonians had an amazing knowledge of what are known to us as Pythagorean triangles, i.e. triangles constructed in such a way that the sum of the squares on two of the sides is equal to the square on the third side. As every schoolboy knows, if these conditions apply, the angle between the two shorter sides must be a right angle.

Three columns of figures are impressed into the tablet and there was originally a fourth, which is now missing. When translated into modern

COUNTING AND THE PRACTICAL USES OF NUMBERS

figures, the second and third columns read as follows:

119	169
3367	4825
4601	6649
12709	18541
65	97
319	481
2291	3541
799	1249
481	769
4961	8161
45	75
1679	2929
161	289
1771	3229
56	106

The first column (not reproduced above) gives a list of ratios which, on investigation, were found to be the ratios between the squares of the numbers in the right hand column and the squares of the missing set of numbers. From the data given, it can be inferred that the complete tablet gave the three sides *in integers* of a set of Pythagorean triangles ABC such that angle ABC is a right angle and angle ACB reduces, in successive triangles, by about one degree from almost 45° to almost 30°.

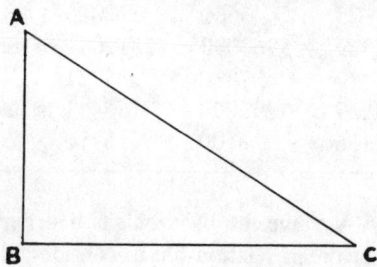

As evidence of their powers of computation, this list is truly astonishing. It would be a laborious, but not intrinsically difficult, task for a modern geometer to provide such a list of the relative lengths of the sides of such triangles, provided that he was able to use decimal approximations for at least one of the sides, but he would certainly feel the need for a computer to search for solutions in which all three sides were expressed in *whole numbers*. For some angles ACB, of course, such solutions are impossible. If angle ACB is 45°, for instance, the ratio between the hypotenuse and either of the other two sides is irrational and cannot be expressed in whole numbers. The Babylonians probably knew this and have not attempted to arrive at a solution which gives an exact number of degrees for the angle.

To show the beauty of the Babylonian table, the integral values of all three sides of each triangle, together with their squares and the value of angle ACB are reproduced below

SIDE BC	SIDE AB	SIDE AC	BC^2	AB^2	AC^2	ANGLE ACB
120	119	169	14400	14161	28561	44°45'
3456	3367	4825	11943936	11336689	23280625	44°15'
4800	4601	6649	23040000	21169201	44209201	43°47'
13500	12709	18541	182250000	161518681	343768681	43°16'
72	65	97	5184	4225	9409	42°5'
360	319	481	129600	101761	231361	41°33'
2700	2291	3541	7290000	5248681	12538681	40°41'
960	799	1249	921600	638401	1560001	39°46'
600	481	769	360000	231361	591361	38°43'
6480	4961	8161	41990400	24611521	66601921	37°26'
60	45	75	3600	2025	5625	36°52'
2400	1679	2929	5760000	2819041	8579041	34°59'
240	161	289	57600	25921	83521	33°51'
2700	1771	3229	7290000	3136441	10426441	33°44'
90	56	106	8100	3136	11236	31°53'

Quite obviously, the ancient Babylonians had explored the possibilities of the Pythagorean relationship in considerable depth millenia before Pythagoras himself came on the scene. This gives us one of the reasons for their choice of 60 as the base of their scientific system of enumeration, since it is a mathematical fact, well-known to them, that if a^2 plus b^2 equals c^2 and a, b and c are all integers, abc *must* be a multiple of 60. It is precisely this fact which enabled the makers of the

COUNTING AND THE PRACTICAL USES OF NUMBERS   79

Plimpton 322 tablet to find suitable integers with which to construct their table.

The simplest Pythagorean triangle was known to both the Babylonians and the Egyptians long before they discovered the laws governing the relationship. It is the triangle with sides of 3, 4 and 5 units, and it will at once be noted that 3 times 4 times 5 is 60. The Egyptians particularly are known from pyramid illustrations to have used a rope with knots dividing it into 12 equal sections to construct a right angle by stretching the rope taut to form a 3—4—5 triangle.

Now the two sides of this triangle containing the right angle have lengths of three and four units respectively, making a neat septenary, divided into the usual ternary and quaternary. This particular triangle gave the ancients much food for speculation, for it forms half of a rectangle which has lunar properties.

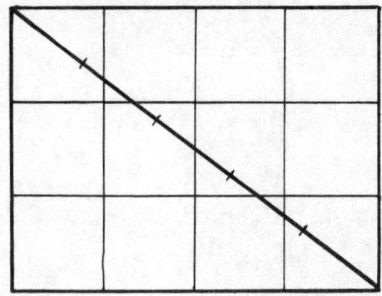

The rectangle naturally has sides of three and four units respectively and so can be divided into three times four smaller rectangles. This is the same number as the total number of units comprising the three sides of the triangle. It is also the number of the months of the year, as seven is the number of days represented by one phase of the moon. This is the rectangle which formed the breastplate of the Hebrew High Priest. Each section was filled by a jewel representing one of the 12 tribes of Israel. In number-philosophy, one would say that the rectangle shows the three principles of creation in their relationship with the four elements of created matter.

For our present purpose, it shows the connection between the important number twelve and the number seven. Twelve is the number of the months of the year, the signs of the Zodiac, the tribes of Israel, the Apostles of Christianity and the hours of the day. The number was, until recently, preserved in Britain and some other countries in the form of pence in a shilling and inches in a foot. Of all its uses, the original and most basic use is in the months of the year. Since the number of lunations in a solar year is never exact, the month must have resulted from an idealisation somewhat removed from the actual lunar month and this brings us to the second, and more decisive, reason for the development of the sexagesimal system.

The Circle and the Year

It is naturally not coincidence that the circle has 360 degrees, the same number as the days of the ancient year. The circle was so divided *because* of the number of days in the year and the number of both was fixed at the time, with intercalary days being added to the basic 360 as necessary to make the start of a new civil year coincide with the start of a new solar year.

To see how this came about, we must go back to the beginnings of astronomical observation and put ourselves in the shoes of the priests whose function it was to determine the dates on which the great fertility festivals of the year should be held.

But there were *no* dates, no clocks, no ways of measuring time at all until these early astronomers made them.

COUNTING AND THE PRACTICAL USES OF NUMBERS   81

They were aware, without measuring, that the length of the daylight period and the dark period of the day varied at different times of the year and that the long days tended to be warm whereas the short days were cold. They were aware that the moon's position among the stars changed by a fixed amount each day and that these changes were in some way related to the moon's phases, since at each new moon the body had moved its position through about a twelfth part of the heavens. The patterns of the fixed stars had long ago been recognised and named and they realised that all the stars appeared to revolve around a fixed point in the sky almost, but not quite, once in a day.

Now without measuring instruments, there was still a great deal of information which could be determined accurately. The first datum points were sunrise and sunset. These points enabled short-term calculations to be made relating the moon's phases to the solar day and the first ratio to be worked out with reasonable accuracy was probably the number of days taken by a complete lunation.

Over a fairly long period, the length of the sidereal year would also be determined as a ratio with the solar day by counting the number of days between the times when a particular star rose or set at the same time as the sun. In Egypt, the star used for this purpose was Sothis (Sirius).

Probably the first actual measuring instrument was that used to determine the four seasonal days, i.e. the spring equinox, midsummer day, autumn equinox and midwinter day. To construct such an instrument, it is first necessary to find the cardinal points of the compass accurately. An earthwork circle would first be made with a perfectly level top to act as an artificial horizon. The levelling of the top was no problem to the ancient Egyptians, who cut a narrow channel in such a construction and filled it with water, cutting away the earth until it was level with the water. The centre of the circle was marked with a chin-high stone and, from this point, all observations were made, with the observer's chin resting on the stone.

It was now possible to determine true north and south with complete accuracy by watching from the centre of the circle for the rising of a particular star and having an assistant mark the circle at the point from which it seemed to rise. Another mark could then be made at the setting point. When the angle between these two points was bisected, the true north-south line resulted.

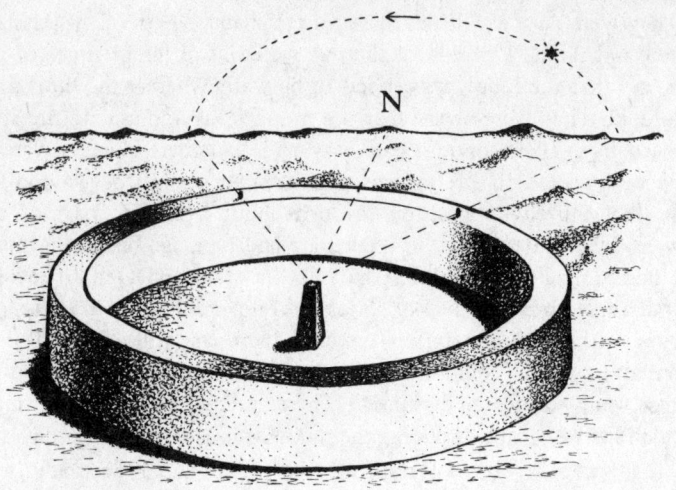

This same structure can now be used to determine:

(a) the equinoxes, when the sun rises and sets exactly east and west,
(b) midsummer day, when the rising and setting points are at their maximum deviation north of east and west, and
(c) midwinter day, when the rising and setting points are at their maximum deviation south of east and west.

This leads to the construction of a shadow-clock, an obelisk, to determine the moment of noon, when the shadow of the obelisk crosses the north-south line.

The hours of the night, however, can only be measured with reference to the stars and so it becomes desirable to plot the positions of the stars accurately. To do this it is necessary to be able to mark the heavens into equal parts, or degrees, but how do we set about this? In our next chapter, we shall take an imaginary journey into the past to see if this question can be answered by those who were first concerned with the problem.

6

The Centre and the Circle

The ancients were, as we have seen, remarkably skilled in astronomy some thousand or so years before Christ. Whether this knowledge had its beginnings in one centre of learning and was then propagated into other lands is immaterial for our present investigation. What we shall now do is to go on a voyage of creative imagination into the ancient past and try to put ourselves into the shoes of one of the men who first attempted to describe the movements of the planets and the stars with quantitative accuracy.

It is sunrise. The first glint of the sun's disc makes its appearance over the distant eastern mountain range. The air is still as though nature held her breath at the moment of birth of a new day. Even the morning song of the birds is stilled during this magic moment.

I stand at a respectful distance watching Adu, the white-robed, white-bearded priest as he makes his morning obeisance to the Source of Life, his arms outstretched and his eyes fixed on the mounting disc.

At last, he lowers his arms and turns in my direction. I bow low before him and he raises his right hand above my head in benediction.

'Welcome, my son,' he says, 'Come, sit beside me on the grass, for I perceive that you have journeyed far to see me. You are not, I think, of this place, nor even of this time.'

I acknowledge the truth of what he says and sit on the grass facing him He looks searchingly into my eyes.

'What is it you seek?' he asks.

'My father,' I answer, 'it has been told in my land and time that you discovered how to measure the movements of the heavens and how to plot the positions of the stars. I would like to know how.'

He raises his hand in a peculiar gesture.

'This knowledge is not for the profane, my son, for they would only debase it. Only those who have prepared themselves by long discipline under the care of a true priest may receive such knowledge as he possesses. Yet, you have journeyed far. . . .'

He meditates for some time; then he turns to me, smiling.

'Prove to me the knowledge you already possess and, if it is adequate, I will grant your wish.'

He proceeds to question me at length about astronomy, arithmetic and geometry. Some of my answers appear to puzzle him, but at length he is satisfied.

'It seems that you have knowledge to which I myself have not yet attained,' he says slowly, 'so how can I hold back that which I do know? Close your eyes.'

When I do as he asks, he lays his hands on my closed eyelids briefly.

'Now, if you sit there quietly, with a quiescent mind, I will tell you of my researches and, as I speak, you will see the scenes from my past which I am describing.

'My master was already old when I became his pupil at the age of 15 years. This is he whom you will now see at the time of my initiation.'

As he speaks, a scene becomes visible to my inner vision. I am in an open cave in a mountainside. It is night and a fire burns in the cave. At one side of the fire sits a venerable, white-robed figure, his old eyes fixed sightlessly on the fire. Opposite him, young Adu is sitting cross-legged; his naked body is marked all over as though he has suffered some ravaging ordeal. His skin shines in the firelight from the soothing oil with which his wounds have been rubbed. His face is, nevertheless, calm and eager as he listens to the old man.

'You have done well, Adu.' The old priest's voice is dry and cracked. 'You have suffered, as all must at initiation, and yet you have shown your absolute trust in my protection. It is good, and you shall be, even as I have been, a leader and a father to the people.

'Now, look through the opening of the cave and tell me what you see.'

The youth turns to face the entrance to the cave. He speaks confidently.

'I see the land of my ancestors lit by the radiance of the moon-mother and I see the stars performing their nightly journey across the sky.'

'Good. Now close your eyes and tell me what you see.'

'I see nothing.'

'No land, no stars, no moon-mother?'

'No, father.'

'Then this is the lesson of your initiation. This is the essence of my knowledge which I now impart to you to carry as long as you live. When you open your eyes, the land and the stars are there before you. When you close them, they are not. You are the centre of the universe and re-create it each time you look at it. Do you accept this?'

'I do, father, for you have shown me that it is so.'

'Then, what creates you?'

The boy stares dumbly. At last, he shakes his head.

'My father, I do not understand. It is said that the land and I myself and all the people come from our mother-moon. Yet you have shown that I re-create these things myself. What is the answer to this riddle?'

The old man smiles his satisfaction. He nods his head several times.

'The dilemma provides its own answer, Adu. When you saw that you re-created these things by seeing them, you did not then assume that you, Adu, are the Supreme Creator. That is as it should be. You recognise that you create, but you know you are also created.

'The answer to the problem is very simple. You are the centre of what you create, but since your creation is a limited one, you are, from a higher viewpoint, a limited centre. That which creates you must therefore be a centre of a higher order. When you look at the moon-mother, you re-create her. When she looks down at you, she re-creates you and all other men, together with their land and all that is in it. From her viewpoint, she is now the centre. But there is another higher centre in our father the Sun, who looks down on ourselves and also our mother-moon and all the planets. And so it goes on; everywhere, the centres re-create each other, but some are greater than others. The hierarchy of creation goes back and back to infinity, each new centre being higher than the one before it until, ultimately, we can imagine the Supreme Centre of all, which creates everything that is.'

He pauses to allow the idea to crystallise in the mind of his pupil. When he speaks again, his voice seems more sonorous as if he is momentarily re-creating his own youth.

'You, Adu, are destined to make great discoveries if you build on this one lesson. All that is created comes from a centre. Find the centre and you automatically find all that the centre creates and the laws by which it is governed.'

The scene fades as I again hear the normal voice of my mentor.

'I have never, for one moment, forgotten the lesson of my initiation,' he says. 'All my researches have started by my asking myself what is the centre which creates the thing I am studying. I watch the merchants counting their goods, for instance, and I ask what Centre creates the numbers that they use.'

A new scene confronts me. The young priest stands in the market place. A seller and a buyer are arguing about the price of a basket of eggs. For the third time, the seller takes all the eggs out of the basket and lays them on the ground. Then he starts to put them back one by one. Each time he puts in an egg, the buyer raises another finger until all ten are raised. Then he makes a mark in the sand, closes his fists and starts again. When all the eggs are in the basket, there are three marks in the sand and he has four fingers raised; there are therefore 34 eggs. The buyer counts out three silver pieces, erasing one mark for each piece. Then he looks at his four raised fingers and, shaking his head, takes four eggs out of the basket and returns them to the seller, who nods his agreement and picks up the silver. The buyer goes off happily with his 30 eggs.

Adu stares at the patch of sand where the marks were. Suddenly, he claps his hands together as if delighted with a new discovery. I hear his voice speaking to me again.

'You see what I was asking myself? What is this thing called number which is used to count objects? It is not something I can see and touch, yet it exists. I can create it in my mind even without objects to count. So what is the Centre which creates the numbers? Suddenly, I see it clearly. The first mark on the ground gives me the clue I seek. It is simply the idea of *oneness*, unity. One itself is the Centre which creates all the other numbers. Where there is one, there is a possibility of two, but without one, two cannot exist.

'We have ten fingers. When we have used all ten, this creates another *one*, the mark in the sand. This *one* creates another order of numbers the same as before, from one to ten, which we can again count on our fingers. We can repeat the process of creating new orders of numbers indefinitely by making one mark in the new order represent ten marks in the order next below it, but all were created from the one raised finger which started the process. So One is the Centre and numbers are its creation.

'This thing which I discovered enabled me to perform calculations with numbers in a short time and with certainty which the merchant you saw would never have been able to do without making errors and that only after many hours of work. For I saw that it is possible to add together higher orders of numbers just as we add numbers of the lowest order.'

A Centre of the Universe

An older Adu sits with three of his brother-priests. He looks radiantly happy and opens his arms as if he would encompass the others with his joy.

'My brethren,' he says, 'rejoice with me, for I have been led to discover the answer to the problem which has engaged all our minds for so long.'

They all lean towards him expectantly.

'You mean the secret of dividing the heavens into equal portions?' one of them asks.

'I mean just that. We have all laboured long to find a way by which we could calculate the movements of the sun, the moon and the planets and so foretell their future positions, but there has always been a difference between our predictions and our observations. The reason for this is that we have been using our straight measuring stick to make sights on the stars and so measure the distances between them. But the equally-spaced notches on the stick do not measure equal spaces in the heavens.

'Why is this so? I could not answer the question and so, as I always do when I cannot find the answer to a problem, I began to meditate upon what my master taught me. I went back in spirit to the very day of my initiation and repeated to myself the great lesson he imparted to me on that day. Immediately, I began to see what was wrong. When I look at the heavens, I am the Centre which re-creates them. If I want to measure them, I must do so from the Centre, but what is measured from a centre? Surely it is a *circle*. And then I saw that any line across the heavens is part of a circle of which I am the centre, and the circle continues below the horizon until it comes up on the other side and so completes itself. When we view the movements of the heavens, we are viewing the movement of a wheel, of which we are the hub.

'But, my brethren, our straight measuring stick is not part of a circle, nor can we measure the circumference of a circle by reference to it.'

Adu picks up a wooden stake and a mallet which have been lying beside him and walks some distance away from the group. He stops and drives the stake into the ground. Divining his intention, one of the

THE CENTRE AND THE CIRCLE

other three leaves them and comes back shortly with a length of rope. He holds one end of the rope on top of the stake, while Adu takes the other end and stretches it out as far as it will go. Then, using the rope as a guide, Adu inscribes a circle in the sand with the stake as its centre.

'I have now drawn a circle by the method known to you all,' he says. 'Let this circle now represent a line right across the heavens, below the horizon and back to the starting point. Do you agree that the representation is just?'

They all assent eagerly.

'Now bring the measuring stick.'

A stick is brought which is divided into ten equal parts by notches.

'Kandu, will you please take the stick and, using it as a sight, we will mark out the circumference of the circle at the points indicated by the notches.'

They proceed to do so, with Kandu calling directions while Adu drives a stake into the ground on the circumference of the circle at each point indicated.

'Brethren,' Adu says to them as soon as the ten stakes are in position, 'I want you to come here and look at the spacing between the stakes. Even without measurement, you can see that the spaces are certainly not equal. Those at the two ends are much smaller than the ones in the middle.'

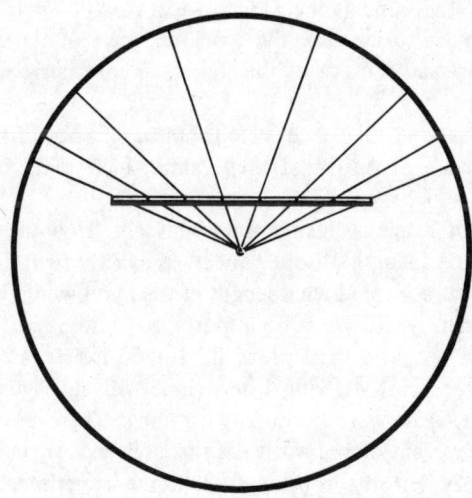

Somewhat shaken, they assent to the truth of Adu's statement. Then Adu pulls up all of the stakes on the circle except one, to which he now points.

'This stake is just one of the points of which the circumference of the circle is composed. In this sense, it was created by the other stake in the centre of the circle. And just as in dealing with numbers, each order of unity acts as a centre for the next higher order, so I am going to let this point act as a centre of a higher order than the original centre of the circle. Kandu, take the same rope we used to draw the circle and hold one end of it on this stake.'

Kandu does so and the rest watch as Adu takes the other end of the rope and stretches it taut, moving round with it until the end is exactly on the circumference. Here he drives in another stake.

'Another Centre!' he says and repeats the process to find the position for the next stake.

With three stakes driven into the circumference, he asks the others to say whether the spacing between them is equal. They agree that it must be exactly equal.

'Now,' Adu exclaims dramatically, 'I am going to show you the truly amazing part of my discovery.'

With Kandu's help, he measures three more spaces round the circumference, driving in stakes at each new point.

'We have measured five spaces altogether and you agree that each space is exactly the same as the others. I want two of you to take the rope and, with it, to measure the remaining part of the circle, that between the first and the last of the stakes, the only part we have not yet measured.'

They do so and, to their utter astonishment, the rope fits the space exactly. They stare at Adu as if they cannot believe the evidence of their own eyes.

'What kind of magic is this?' Kandu whispers. 'How did you know that I would bring a length of rope which was exactly right?'

'I neither knew nor cared what length of rope you would bring,' Adu answers triumphantly. 'It was of no importance to the result.'

'But it *must* be and I shall prove it.' Kandu insists. He cuts off a length of the rope and, drawing a new circle with it, begins to repeat the experiment. Adu watches quietly, smiling. There are shouts of disbelief as, once again, the rope divides the circle exactly into six equal parts. Again they cut the rope and again the experiment produces

THE CENTRE AND THE CIRCLE

exactly the same result. In the end, convinced, they look at each other in wonder and then, as if by common consent, move over towards Adu and prostrate themselves before him. But he rebukes them sharply.

'Brethren, enough! Am I a god that you should prostrate yourselves? I am no different from you, but thanks to the wise guidance of my master, I believe I have discovered one of the laws by which the universe was created. As befits a first-order creation of the Supreme One, it is a thing of surpassing beauty and utter simplicity.'

He repeats the experiment in miniature in a small patch of sand in front of him, so that they can see the resulting figure clearly.

'Observe the perfect symmetry of the figure. Each mark is equidistant from its two neighbours on the circumference and from the centre of the circle. These seven marks are surely worthy to be, for us, the eternal symbol of the creative activity of the Supreme One.'

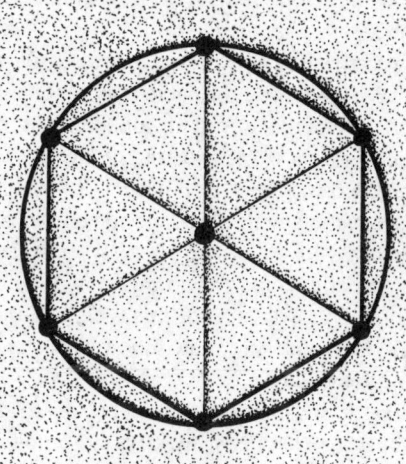

The eyes of Kandu light up suddenly.

'Why yes,' he exclaims, 'it *is* the perfect symbol. The six points on the circumference represent the created universe while the seventh point in the centre represents the Creator. And I am convinced that the symbol itself was created by God himself for us all to see if we were not so blind.'

He beckons them to follow him and runs towards the back of the nearby temple. Lifting the lid of a wooden box standing on a trestle behind the building, he points wordlessly inside. A steady buzzing sound comes from within. The others look inside the hive and see a honeycomb. It is composed entirely of perfectly symmetrical six-sided cells, each with its bee in the centre busily 'creating' honey.

The Symbol and the Planets

Fanciful as the preceding sections have been, I believe the ideas they incorporate represent, in essence, the trigger leading to the sacred status of the septenary in its 'planetary' aspect. The division of the circle into six equal segments with radii as chords must have been among the first empirical discoveries relating to the geometry of the circle. It was also responsible for a great deal of the initial symbolism attached to other numbers.

The circle was obviously the most important figure for an astronomer and so it was almost certainly the astronomer-priests who first made the discovery.

Thousands of years before Copernicus expressed the view which was considered heretical in his time, the ancient astronomers knew that the sun was the centre of the solar system and that the planets revolved around it. The 'planets' they knew were the moon, Mercury, Venus, Mars, Jupiter and Saturn. Is it not natural that they should have connected these six planets with the six points on the circumference of the circle and the sun with its centre? If they considered it at all, the earth was seen as something apart from this system. It was simply their observation platform. The evidence for this is clear in the naming of the days of the week after the sun, the moon and the five naked-eye planets. There is no Earth-day.

The mundane week was naturally projected on to the Divine Week of creation. Note again that only six days are applied to the active creating of the world, the seventh being a non-active day on which the Creator returns to his point of rest at the centre of the circle of His creation. The biblical creation story in the form we have it is clear evidence of the significance of the six-pointed division of the circle, especially when it is remembered that the ideas behind it were handed down to the Hebrews by the Mesopotamians whose priests were the most likely discoverers of the process.

This is also the origin of the sacred symbol of the Jews, the six-pointed star.

THE CENTRE AND THE CIRCLE

Having discovered the method, the first thing the astronomers would do would be to construct a sighting circle based on the six divisions and set it up in line with the rotation of the stars. It would then not take them long to find out that, if they watched the position of a particular star at the same time every evening, its position would change through one complete division in almost exactly the time taken for two complete lunations. And so they would divide each segment in two 'houses' which, projected on to the heavens, became the signs of the Zodiac and, in terms of time, became the months of the year. From this to the division of each 'house' into 30 degrees, each representing one day of time, is but a short step. All this, of course, involves some compromise and approximation, for a lunation is less than 30 days. Neither the 360 days of the final division nor the 12 idealised lunations are equal to a solar year, the former being short by five days and the latter by nine. The lunations come back approximately into line after 10 years, but the only way in which the 360-day year could be kept in step with the solar year was to add a thirteenth five-day month each year. This extra month belonged to nothing and was an unfortunate flaw in the symmetry of the system.

Gradually, the thirteenth month began to be considered unlucky and it was dangerous to do anything on the five intercalary days. Later, this feeling would become attached to the number thirteen itself and this is the origin of the idea that one of the thirteen present at the Last Supper was an evil supernumary.

We have already shown how the Pythagorean triangle produces multiples of 60, making it easier to do the calculations involved using number to a base of 60 instead of 10. The division of the circle into 360 degrees made a 60-base counting system almost essential for the complicated calculations which had to be carried out by the astronomers. Moreover, the base itself is divisible by 1,2,3,4,5,6,10,12,15, 20 and 30, whereas the base 10 is only divisible by 1,2 and 5. This gives the sexagesimal system tremendous flexibility, of which the astronomers made full use.

7

Involution and Evolution

We have suggested that the initial impetus of the idea of the four elements, earth, water, air and fire, occurred in the world catastrophe when the images of the heaving earth, engulfing waters, rushing air and consuming fire were indelibly burned into the consciousness of the survivors as primeval matter in torment. In the stable form in which they are examined by the philosophers, however, the four elements do have an obvious and valid correspondence with reality, for we know matter in three forms or states; solid, liquid and gaseous, corresponding to earth, water and air and it is heat or 'fire' which converts one into another, melting solids and evaporating liquids. If we understand the elements in this way, they are strictly rational and the classification is perfectly scientific. We neither know matter, nor can we imagine it in any other than the three forms mentioned and *any* transmutation of matter from one state to any other is accompanied by the absorption or liberation of heat.

Actually, this applies strictly only to terrestrial matter, because, if we journey out among the stars, we shall, here and there, find matter in another state, which we can describe as 'collapsed'. In bodies which are in this state, the actual structure of the atoms has changed so that they are not, as in ordinary matter, relatively far apart and held at a distance by the forces within each atom, but are jammed tightly together so that one cubic centimetre of such matter may have a mass of 500 tons. The astronomers tell us that there are dark bodies in the universe which are smaller than the earth but which have a mass equal to 100 suns. By comparison with this collapsed state, what we call solid matter seems almost like empty space. This thought points to another state in which matter is known to exist. It is the matter of interstellar space, for space is rarely completely empty but contains clouds of very sparse matter — matter as much more rarified than the gaseous state as collapsed matter is more 'packed' than the solid state with which we are familiar.

The only basic difference between the various states of matter is the relative closeness and freedom of movement of the molecules. In solid matter, the molecules are bound together fairly tightly and the only relative movement is one of vibration, the frequency of which is determined by the atomic mass and the structure of the bonds between the molecules, while the intensity of the vibration is a measure of the temperature of the body. If more heat is applied, the vibrations of the molecules increase until a stage is reached when the energy of the vibrations becomes greater than the cohesion of the inter-molecular bonds and individual molecules are able to 'change partners' with relative freedom. In this state, which we know as the liquid state, we can compare the molecules to dancers moving in lines in opposite directions, each grasping the hand of the dancer nearest to him in passing and then moving on to the next. If we excite the molecules still further by continuing to apply heat, their vibrations will become so great as to overcome even the 'hand-grasping'. The molecules now break away from each other completely, providing they are given room to move, and rush about in a completely haphazard manner, continually colliding with each other and rebounding. This is the gaseous state and it is the 'bombardment' of the molecules which is responsible for the pressure exerted by a gas in an enclosed space, e.g. inside a party balloon.

The above is a crude representation of the molecular view of matter, but we do not need either instruments or mathematical calculations to determine which state of matter we are dealing with in practice. If an object is relatively constant in shape, we say it is solid; if it flows, seeking the lowest level in whatever contains it and settling down with a flat upper surface, we say it is liquid; if it becomes invisible and only reveals its presence by its smell or its pressure on an object moved rapidly through it, we say it is gaseous.

Such descriptions are, however, only approximate, for it is possible to produce a powder so fine that it flows like a liquid. Glass, on the other hand, is actually liquid in form although it remains visibly fixed in shape. There are also many intermediate, but quite stable, states, such as the semi-liquid state of heavy oils or of molasses. Nor is the amount of heat needed to turn matter from the solid to the liquid state, or from the liquid to the gaseous state, constant. At ordinary temperatures, mercury is a liquid and it takes a great deal of work to remove enough heat from the metal to solidify it. Water, however, can be turned from the solid state (ice) to the liquid state and thence to the gaseous state by moving it through a comparatively small range of temperatures.

In spite of these considerations, there is usually no doubt in our minds about the classification of the objects with which we are familiar into solid, liquid and gaseous, or a mixture of two or more of these states.

As the ancient philosophers were quick to recognise, the four elements are vital to the existence of man. His body-structure is solid, so it is the equivalent of earth; he needs a constant flow of blood (water) to nourish the tissues and remove impurities and a flow of air into and out of his lungs to rejuvenate the blood. His body temperature has to be maintained within quite a narrow range to enable the processes of his metabolism to proceed.

It is not surprising that the sun has always been the symbol of the life-giver. Imagine what would happen if the earth were to be removed into outer space far from the influence of the sun. In a very short time, all the accumulated heat would dissipate, the seas would solidify and the very air would first form a liquid layer on the earth's surface and then solidify. In the end, matter would exist only in the solid state and the earth would be completely dead. So the sun is the representative of the creative heat which maintains the 'fire' of matter.

Nevertheless, its influence is not entirely beneficent. Suppose now that the earth were to move into an orbit close to the surface of the sun. The energy of vibration of the molecules of the air would quickly become so great that the air would escape the earth's gravitational pull; the seas would quickly evaporate; the very earth on which we stand would melt and eventually also evaporate. In short, the earth would soon disappear into the gaseous state. And so we say that, although the sun's heat is necessary, so is its opposite, cold. A balance between heat and cold is needed to maintain the states of matter. Heat and cold, being opposites, can be said to annihilate each other; we must therefore invoke a third force to maintain comparative equilibrium without annihilation and this is the principle of *order* If the creative principle of heat is represented by the sun at the centre of the circle and the creative principle of cold is represented by outer space at the periphery of the circle, the third principle, that of order, is represented by the circle itself. The orbital motion of the earth around the sun is a condition of 'free-fall' which keeps us just far enough away from the sun to maintain the balance between the heat of the sun and the cold of

INVOLUTION AND EVOLUTION

outer space. It is this circular motion which we recognise as the *order* of the universe.

Thus we see a visible demonstration of the three principles of creation leading to the four states of matter, one of which (fire) is the 'odd-man-out'. In its ideal form, this is the sacred septenary, built up of the creative ternary and the created quaternary.

From a higher viewpoint, however, the 'many' is still the One, and this can be demonstrated in a very simple way by examining the principles and elements of which the septenary is composed.

First we notice that the four elements do not signify things which are essentially different from each other. The solid, liquid and gaseous states of matter are simply different levels of excitation of the molecules, which depends on the amount of 'fire' they contain and, conversely, their relative state of excitation *is* the 'fire'. So matter is one in essence.

Similarly, when we look at the principle of order, we find that circular motion and spin are universal in application. The galaxies spin on their axes and revolve around each other as do the planets and their satellites. This is analogous to the state of the electrons whose motion in an atom can only be described as orbiting if a mechanistic picture is to be provided. When we speak of the vibrations of heat, we are probably talking about a circular, rather than a back-and-forth motion, for, mathematically, the vibration represented by a sine-wave is a simple projection of motion in a circle.

The fact is that heat cannot be distinguished from vibration and vibration cannot be distinguished from circular motion.

When we treated heat and cold as two opposing principles, we were looking at them from the point of view of an observer midway between the extremes, but there is a continuous gradation from extreme heat to extreme cold. Cold is, therefore, not something positive; it is simply the *absence* of heat.

And so we see that even the three principles are not really different from each other but are three facets of the One, viewed from 'outside'.

There remains only the philosophical distinction between that which creates and that which is created. This is the final polarity, the dualism which appears to separate God from His creatures. It is the basis of the dichotomy of matter and spirit and the stumbling-block to the realisation of the principle of 'As above, so below'. Is it a *real* distinction or one which we impose on reality by reason of the limitations of our thinking?

Let us admit at the outset that we are really asking the question 'What is God?' This is a question which, by its very nature, has no answer. If we try to trace the Creator logically through His creation, we come to a point where the principles of creation are reconciled in their essential unity and are therefore no longer a possible object of rational thought. From our side of the Veil, the idea of God-in-Himself looks like *nothing*. Logically, however, a true void cannot be the Source of anything, so this view of the Creator must be false.

We are compelled to fall back on analogy to provide a partial answer to our question. The analogy we have to use is that based on the notion of selfhood. I am a centre of awareness, but if I strip away from myself everything which is an *object* of my awareness, the world around me, my own body and even my own thoughts and imaginings, I am left with nothing, in the sense of *no thing*. My selfhood is not a thing. It has no place of location in space and time. Yet I do not doubt that it *is*. I can only say that it is a point of reference from which all things and all ideas are viewed. It is outside space and time but creates these qualities for itself. *From the point of view of this one self*, the world does not exist without the self's awareness of it. Can I then say that the matter of which the world is composed is of a different nature from my immaterial self? I cannot do so. I live in the world, but, equally, the world lives in me. I say that this desk on which I am writing is solid because I can *see* its constant outline and *feel* the resistance of its surface beneath my hand. But traced back to their ultimate meaning, these sense impressions are images appearing in my awareness or, in other words, are ordered patterns within myself.

Now I apply this analogy to the Source of all being. In a sense, to do so is to 'create God in the image of man', but it is the nearest one can come to an answer. If creation is purposeful, it implies that the Creator is essentially a Self, albeit what I understand by selfhood expanded to infinity. This being so, matter is not something different from its Creator. If it is denied that creation is purposeful, all the sceptic is doing is to describe the principles of creation as an inevitable process leading to matter and again it must be concluded that the principles and their results are not essentially different.

So the best answer which can be given is that there are not two opposed ideas, of the Creator on the one hand and the created universe on the other. They are One and the septenary is effectively unity in the same way that the Trinity is a Unity.

When this has been said, it leaves us still where we were, in the world of appearances, involved with matter as though it was something different from ourselves with which we are tied up. We may destroy our involvement intellectually but in terms of experience it is real enough. This is why the process of involution is seen as a 'fall' into the material, while the returning process of evolution, the toil of stripping away one illusion after another, is seen as a climb back up to the Real.

The Cross and the Elements
One reason for the innate force of the cross as a symbol is its emotional, instinctual and rational application to the state of involvement with matter.

The symbol of the cross is primarily a representation of the earth, by reference to the four points of the compass. Its secondary significance refers to matter in general, conceived as the four elements. Many subsidiary meanings have been grafted on to the cross by making various adjustments to its shape and ornamentation, but we are concerned, at this stage, with the simple form, two straight lines, one vertical and one horizontal, crossing at their mid-points.

If the cross had no greater symbolic meaning than that of a visual 'name' for earth, it would not have been considered sacred for thousands of years. The fact is that, as a symbol, it is ambivalent in the extreme. Consider, for instance, its Christian symbolism, where it stands for the agony of crucifixion alongside the glory of salvation.

Laid flat on the ground, it may stand for simple orientation which, in turn, is a symbol of order and conformity in nature, or it may equally well stand for the diametrically-opposed idea of indecision, the unresolved choice of the crossroads.

In folklore, a crossroads has an ominous significance. Just as the pious dead are buried beneath a vertical cross, to act as a pointer to heaven, those who are assumed to have renounced the faith, such as witches, are buried at a crossroads with a stake driven through the heart to pin down the evil spirit. Dogs were sacrificed to Hecate, the evil feminine principle, at a crossroads. Hecate was the triform goddess of the dead, who taught witchcraft and sorcery, in both of which a perverted form of sexuality was believed to play a large part. The supine cross is also a symbol of perverted sexuality since it combines two phallic symbols in such a way that one penetrates the other.

The cross was probably the first significant mark made by man and was the forerunner of all alphabetic writing. Hence, the name of the Hebrew letter Taw, originally written 'X', means simply 'mark'. This letter has retained its basic form of two lines crossing each other ever since alphabetic writing was invented, the only changes made having been its orientation from oblique to vertical and, in the capital form, the moving of the horizontal line to the top of the vertical line in the Roman and Greek alphabets.

If the cross represents earth, it is also a symbol of the World-axis, the Centre at which the 'two worlds' meet and the point at which the soul of man may meet God. This is partly due to its being a crude representation of a tree and, hence, of the Tree of Life and partly because, in its 'outgoing' aspect, it shows the effect of polarity in two dimensions, while in its 'returning' aspect, it symbolises the union of the opposites.

It is probably because of its inherent simplicity that the cross is capable of carrying so many different levels of meaning. Numerically, for instance, it may be considered as the marker of a point, the centre where the lines cross, and therefore to represent the One, but it is also the union of two lines, giving it a binary character, while the crossroads in particular is a ternary symbol (this is why it is sacred to Hecate), the idea being that one is supposed to be already on one of the roads and is now faced with a choice of three roads to follow. As an earth-symbol, it is a quaternary, but as a symbol of man, it is fivefold (representing the five senses), the centre being included in the number as it is in the case of the three-dimensional cross which represents the septenary.

The three-dimensional cross and what is known as the Calvary cross aptly show the difference between the septenary considered as 6 plus 1 and as 3 plus 4 respectively. The three-dimensional cross points to the four corners of the earth plus 'up' and 'down' and thus represents the whole manifested universe radiating from the Centre. The Centre may be seen as the Creator or as the consciousness of man, made 'in the image of God'. This dual viewpoint is also possible in the case of the 'planetary' septenary with its Centre and its six points on the circumference of the circle.

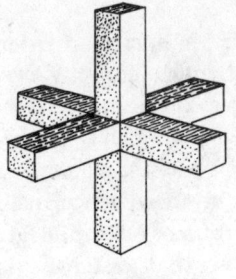 

The Calvary cross represents the 3 plus 4 septenary, as does the pyramid. It consists of a cross mounted on a base of three steps. The name of this form suggests that the steps are intended to signify the hill upon which the Crucifixion took place, but the original designer was, consciously or unconsciously, motivated by a deeper idea. Expressed in Christian terms, this is the idea that, while the materiality of Jesus was sacrificed on the cross, the Christ in him was the unmoved participant in the Triunity of Godhead. In more general terms, the symbol shows, in its involutionary aspect, matter manifested as a result of the three principles, which it contains as its base and, in its evolutionary aspect, the possibility of 'mounting' to the 'sacrifice' of the material man through the resolving and reconciliation not only of the opposites (as seen in the cross itself) but even of the very principles of creation, for this is the final Initiation, the return to and realisation of the One.

The anserated cross of Egyptian hieroglyphics represents a similar set of ideas in a different form. In writing, the sign was the determinative for words referring to living things, hence its accepted meaning of 'life', but it is also a combination of the male and female, active and passive signs, and thus illustrates the balance of polarities necessary for the maintenance of life at all levels. Procreation, for instance, is the union of the male (cross) and the female (circle), while matter is the union of spatial dimensions (cross) and temporal duration (circle). These are also the philosophical ideas behind the problem known as 'squaring the circle' and may have motivated the pyramid designers to evolve a pyramid shape in which the perimeter of the square base is equal to the circumference of the circle whose radius is equal to the height of the pyramid.

The Wheel of Life

The similarity has been pointed out between human evolution and the passage of a ray of light through the relativistic universe. Viewed from a higher dimension, both are in the process of returning to the Centre from which they started. This Centre (with a capital C) has been called the circle whose centre is everywhere and whose circumference is at a point. This sounds like a typical piece of mystico-poetic paradox but, if relativity theory is true, it is an apt description of scientific fact, for the theory tells us that the effect of the presence of matter is to impart a 'curve' to space.

This idea of curved space requires a fourth dimension as a frame of reference within which it can be described mathematically, but it is possible to show the basic idea by means of a three-dimensional illustration. We are to imagine a giant balloon on which lives a tiny flea. Unlike ordinary fleas, this one cannot jump; he is constructed in such a way that he is conscious only of the two-dimensional world represented by the surface of the balloon. The expression 'out into space' for our flea means any direction on the surface of the balloon. Thus, he knows only of the directions forward, backward, right and left and can attribute no meaning to the expressions 'up' and 'down', which to him are mathematical abstractions invented by the two-dimensional mathematicians to explain certain otherwise inexplicable phenomena of his world.

The flea decides to head out into space, and, leaving a dropping to mark his position, crawls straight ahead. On and on he goes in a straight line until at last he bumps his two-dimensional head against the two-dimensional dropping which marked the start of his journey. By heading straight out into space, he has returned to his starting point. From our superior position in the three-dimensional world, we say that he has simply crawled right around the balloon and that, *whatever direction he had started to follow*, he was bound to come back to his starting point provided only that he kept on in a 'straight line'. To the flea, however, the phenomenon can only be explained in terms of higher mathematics, the relativity theory of the two-dimensional mathematicians.

This, say the relativists, is an exact analogy of our own three-dimensional space situation.

This, say the mystic-philosophers, is an exact analogy of the evolution of man. In whatever direction his evolutionary path is

INVOLUTION AND EVOLUTION

headed, it is going towards the Centre from which he emerged in the beginning. However, the evolutionary path of the individual is rarely a straight one; just as everything in the material universe is in constant circular motion, so the cycles of life of the individual man are like small orbits round subsidiary centres. He is born, grows, decays and dies time after time, and his evolutionary path therefore most closely resembles a spiral, but one which carries him inevitably closer and closer towards his final Goal.

This is the idea behind the Wheel of Life, the Zodiac (from the Greek *zoe* — life and *diakos* — wheel). This symbolic wheel is a direct production of the insight of the ancient astronomer-priests, who saw in the motions of the heavens an analogy with the evolutionary journey of man. Like man, the sun was born, rose to splendour, dropped towards the horizon and suffered 'death' daily, only to be born again the next morning after travelling through the underworld. Like man, the moon waxed and waned each month, as did the seasons each year in time with the passage of the stars through the heavens. This symbol has been familiar to the peoples of many lands for thousands of years in forms which change surprisingly little in different places and times. It is always circular in form, almost always has twelve divisions and usually shows correspondences with the seven planets.

Three factors are involved in the division of the Zodiac into twelve 'houses'. The first is the approximate correspondence of the lunations in each year with one twelfth of the total movement of the fixed stars due to the earth's orbital motion. The second is the geometric division of the circle by means of the compasses. The third, and most important, relates directly to the septenary, for each house represents the union of one of the three principles of creation with one of the four elements of matter.

In astrological parlance, the three principles become 'modes' and are called cardinal, fixed and mutable respectively, while the elements retain their ordinary names. The following are the twelve signs with their correspondences.

SIGN	NAME	MODE	ELEMENT
♈	Aries	Cardinal	Fire
♉	Taurus	Fixed	Earth
♊	Gemini	Mutable	Air

SEVEN, THE NUMBER OF CREATION

SIGN	NAME	MODE	ELEMENT
♋	Cancer	Cardinal	Water
♌	Leo	Fixed	Fire
♍	Virgo	Mutable	Earth
♎	Libra	Cardinal	Air
♏	Scorpio	Fixed	Water
♐	Sagittarius	Mutable	Fire
♑	Capricorn	Cardinal	Earth
♒	Aquarius	Fixed	Air
♓	Pisces	Mutable	Water

So the primary attribute of the symbol of the Zodiac is that its twelve signs stand in direct relationship with the septenary. The Wheel of Life is divided by the cross or square into four sections, each containing the same three 'modes', and by the equilateral triangle into three sections, each containing the same four elements.

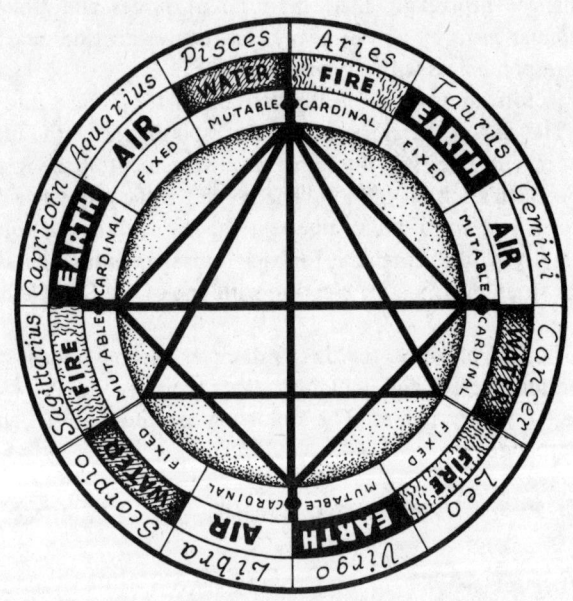

INVOLUTION AND EVOLUTION

We have, of course, met this combination of the cross and triangle before in an alchemical context, and there its character was emphasised by the addition of the figures 3 and 4 to the design which, it was stated, referred to the seven planets and their metals. Here, the same design gives us the key to the arrangement of the twelve houses of the Zodiac.

In traditional astrology, each of the planets 'rules' one or more signs of the Zodiac, the sun and moon each having one sign while all the rest have two each.

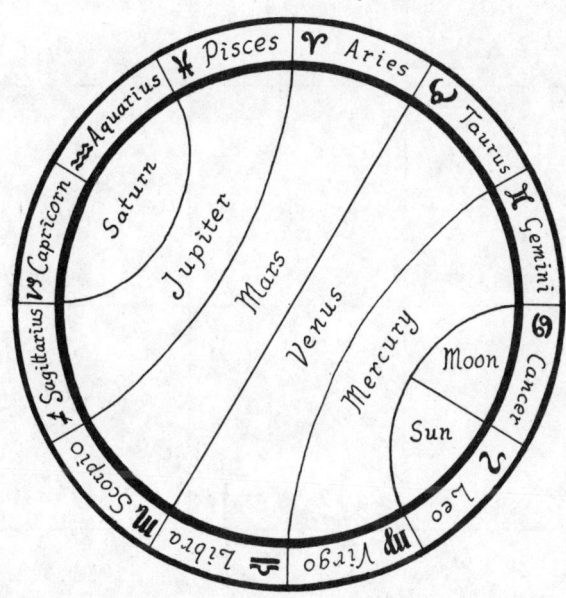

The Symbolism of the Signs of the Zodiac
The imagination has to be stretched to the utmost to visualise in the actual stellar arrangements or constellations the figures suggested by the names of the twelve houses. In the diagram below, the constellations are shown as they appear in a star atlas, the relative brightness of each star being roughly indicated by the size of the dot in the diagram.

Aries	Taurus	Gemini
Cancer	Leo	Virgo
Libra	Scorpio	Sagittarius
Capricorn	Aquarius	Pisces

By joining the stars by lines in certain ways, it is possible to make a figure with some resemblance to the creature it is supposed to represent but, using the same stars, it would be equally possible to make them resemble almost any other creature by the same technique. The evidence strongly suggests that the signs were chosen not for their supposed resemblance to the star-patterns but because each symbolised a particular state or position on the evolutionary path.

INVOLUTION AND EVOLUTION

Aries – the Ram

Since Aries has always been the first of the twelve signs, we should expect it to refer to the first movement of creation. In Hindu symbolism, the ram represents the Parabrahman, the undivided One. For the ancient Egyptians, the ram was the symbol of Amon-Ra, the creator sun-god. Considered in relation to the preceding and following signs, Pisces representing the primordial waters and Taurus representing the life-force, Aries is seen to be the emergence of the first directed energy of creation from the Void. In relation to the human state, it is the first glimmering of individuality. The horns of the ram symbolise the process by which creation takes place, the separation of the opposites, a symbol which reappears in Taurus, so that the two signs together produce 'vertical' and 'horizontal' polarisation, necessary for the appearance of the four elements.

Taurus – the Bull

The Bull represents the driving force behind fertility. Aries also has sexual connotations, but in Taurus the sexual force is dominant. If Aries represents the emergence of individuality from undifferentiated Unity, Taurus represents the urge towards the creation of the 'many'. Central to the mysteries of Mithra is the idea that the sacrifice of the bull enables all life on earth to emerge.

Gemini – the Twins

The Twins show the completion of the creative process of polarisation. They are twins and not just two individuals, to show that the opposites are not essentially different things but are two facets of the same reality. The Gemini also represent the third principle of creation which maintains in being what has been produced by polarisation.

Cancer – the Crab

The Crab, because of its many legs and its circular form, refers to the appearance of the 'many' as a result of the creative principles. In relation to the individual, it represents the infinite number of directions which his evolution can take and suggests the moment of choice of each individual for his incarnation. Its symbolic form shows clearly the centripetal force created by the juxtaposition of the opposites in the world of form.

Leo – the Lion

The Lion is creation 'flexing its muscles'. The creature feels itself to be whole, a complete individual, capable of conquering the world. It is the male force, the will to act in the world. At this point in his evolution, man sees himself as self-sufficient and his life-purpose as the satisfaction of his own desires by the domination of his environment.

Virgo – the Virgin

If Leo is the masculine force, Virgo is its opposite, the passive female manifestation. The existence of Leo *demands* the existence of its opposite. In human evolution, it is the swing of the pendulum from the outgoing to the withdrawing, which takes place continuously on the evolutionary spiral. Virginity, in this case, represents pure passivity. There is, as yet, no sign of the recognition of the possibility of the *conjunctio oppositorum*. This is the nadir of the 'fall into matter', beyond which any movement is the beginning of a returning process. The involution of the individual is complete; the spirit is virgin territory, awaiting its awakening to bestir itself to start on its long journey home.

Libra — the Scales

The seventh sign of the Zodiac is the first in the 'returning' half of the circle. It signifies the 'moment of truth' in which the soul, plunged deep into its involvement with matter, begins to evaluate itself and to recognise that there is something stirring within itself which aspires to a higher state of being. This is the process of self-recognition in which man sees clearly the opposing forces in his own nature, but asserts that he possesses potentially an individuality in which these opposites are capable of being reconciled. In other words, this is the first emergence of spirituality in the creature. The sign also has sexual implications, for, as the symbol suggests, this is also the moment of recognition that the individual soul is a union of both male and female principles. That there is a connection between conscious sexuality and spirituality is an idea common to many cultures and is strongly suggested in the biblical story of the Tree of Knowledge of Good and Evil in the Garden of Eden.

Scorpio — the Scorpion

The Scorpion is also a sexual symbol but represents sex in its negative aspect, being connected with the sting of death. The psychiatrists have made much of this connection, which is probably the origin of the equation of sex and sin in some religious systems. It is said to arise because, at the moment of orgasm, the individual feels as completely helpless as at the moment of death. On the cycle of evolution, it is the realisation that sexuality without spiritual union is a retarding factor. On the other hand, it contains the mystical idea that, in the union of the opposite sides of his nature, the little self is to be sacrificed for the sake of the emergence of the greater Self in the birth of the whole Man. This is reflected in the Christian concept that the man who wants life must first lose it; he must die to be born again.

Sagittarius – the Archer or Centaur

This sign represents the emergence of spirit from the purely material. The figure of the Archer itself shows the triune nature of man; the horse part of the Centaur representing his animal nature and the bow and arrow being the representation of his spiritual nature. The evolving man, at this point, sees his Goal far ahead and begins to move confidently towards it.

Capricorn – the Goat

Like the Centaur, the Capricorn is a union of ideas, in this case, the body of a goat with the tail of a fish. This represents the choice with which the Whole Man is faced, to go on towards the mountains, the true home of the goat, and so complete his union with the divine in the final annihilation of the lower self or to return to the waters of Pisces and so re-enter the Wheel of Life in another incarnation.

Aquarius – the Water Carrier

The Water Carrier pours waters from two vessels so that they mingle. Clearly, this symbolises the reconciliation of the opposites and the return to the state of equilibrium to which the waters of Pisces refer. At one level, the symbol signifies the end of an incarnation and the temporary return to the pre-emergent state; at the evolutionary level, it refers to the individual who has completed his return to the Source and allows his Self to rejoin the ocean of the Great Self; at the cosmic level, it is the withdrawal of matter from manifestation into the 'night of Brahma', from which it will re-emerge in the creation of a new cosmic age. Its correspondence with the Flood is obvious.

Pisces – the Fishes

The two fishes show the dual nature of this sign as being the final dissolution of the individual at the end of a cycle of evolution (equivalent in the cosmic sense to the end of an age) and the potentiality of his re-emergence into a new cycle. These are the primeval waters in which the principles of creation are once again in equilibrium. The symbol clearly shows the Trinity of principles with the two opposites bound together by the third principle. Pictorially, the two fishes are always shown facing in opposite directions, towards the cycle just completed and the new one about to begin. It is interesting to note that, in religious symbolism, the incarnation of an avatar or saviour is often signified by a fish. This is the symbol of Vishnu in India, of Oannes (as man-fish) in Chaldea and even of Christ among the earliest Christians.

Like all symbols, the signs of the Zodiac are capable of interpretation at very many levels, upon which we have only touched to show the interconnection of the whole system in relation to our main theme.

The Tree of Life and the Tarot

Numerical symbolism reaches its most complicated form in the philosophy of the Cabala, with which is associated the ancient pack of cards known as the Tarot. The former system was the creation of a sect of Jewish mystics who emerged in the 13th century. As is well known, the Hebrews used the letters of their alphabet to represent numerals and, from this fact, a system of correspondences and biblical reinterpretation was built up, based on the numerical equivalence of names and words when the number-values of the letters were added together.

The Hebrew alphabet consists of 22 letters, each of which is named after some familiar object. Some of the letters have a different form when they appear at the end of a word, this final form having a different numerical value.

It can be seen from the table which follows that the original correspondence of the numbers and letters was chosen, not for any symbolic equivalence, but simply in sequence according to the order in which the alphabet would normally be recited (hence the obvious correspondence with the usual order of our own alphabet). However, even in biblical times, the Jews attached importance to the numerical significance of the letters, as is shown by the passage in Revelation referring to the number of the Beast.

LETTER	NAME	EQUIVALENT	MEANING	NUMBER-VALUE
א	Aleph	A	Bull	1
ב	Beth	B	House	2
ג	Gimel	G	Camel	3
ד	Daleth	D	Door	4
ה	Heh	H	Window	5
ו	Vaw	V,W	Nail	6
ז	Zain	Z	Sword	7
ח	Cheth	Ch	Field	8
ט	Teth	T	Snake	9
י	Yod	Y	Hand	10
כ	Kaph	K	Curve	20
ל	Lamed	L	Ox-goad	30
מ	Mem	M	Water	40
נ	Nun	N	Fish	50
ס	Samekh	S	Tent-peg	60
ע	Ayin	O	Eye	70
פ	Peh	P	Mouth	80
צ	Tzaddi	TS	Fish-hook	90
ק	Qoph	Q	Head (back)	100
ר	Resh	R	Face	200
ש	Shin	SH	Tooth	300
ת	Taw	T	Mark	400
ך	Kaph – final form			500
ם	Mem – final form			600
ן	Nun – final form			700
ף	Peh – final form			800
ץ	Tzaddi – final form			900

The Tetragrammaton, the sacred name of God, which was never to be pronounced by a Jew, was written as Yod, Heh, Vaw, Heh (hence Jehovah or Yahweh) and had the numerical value of 26; therefore any other name or word with the value of 26 was divine in origin. Similar equivalences were established between all kinds of names and phrases occurring in the Bible and the Cabalists read into the scriptures esoteric meanings related to the numerical values, which they maintained had been deliberately used by the original scribes or had been divinely inspired.

The Cabalists were considerably influenced by the Gnostics and conceived of the Creator, man and the universe as a system of 10 dynamic spheres, for 10 was the number of the first letter of the Tetragrammaton; it was also the base of the number system and therefore the number from which all others were created. This system of spheres is laid out in the form of a diagram, known as the Tree of Life, in which the spheres are connected by 22 paths, equivalent to the 22 letters of the alphabet.

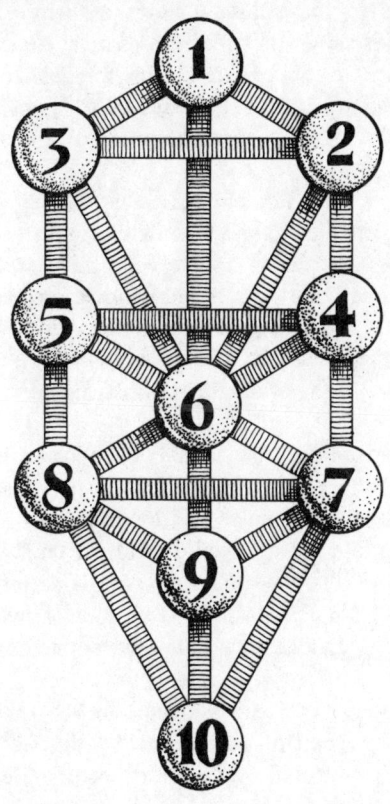

Not only was the Tree considered to show the process of creation, but it was also the symbol of a mystic path back to the Source of Being, along which the adept was able to travel in meditation.

The 10 spheres correspond in many ways with the signs of the Zodiac and with the symbols of the planetary gods. Their arrangement on the Tree can be viewed as a triad plus a septenary and this extension of the septenary of creation to a full decade is an interesting philosophical variant.

The upper Triad consists of the spheres numbered 1, 2 and 3. No. 1 is called Kether, which means 'crown' and the Cabalists knew this as the sphere of primal will. The sphere is thus intended to refer to the One, the Self-Existent, in Whom the will to create must reside. No. 2 is Chokmah, meaning 'wisdom', and No. 3 is Binah, which means 'understanding'. These two are also known as the Father and Mother. The traditional colours of these three spheres are white, grey and black respectively and this shows that they are assumed to stand apart from the direct process of creation. The Cabalists appear to have visualised the One developing the three attributes of will, wisdom and understanding as a preliminary to the emergence of the creative ternary proper.

The real 'descent' into matter takes place in the septenary of the spheres from No. 4 to No. 10 and the interesting feature of this section of the Tree is that it centres on sphere No. 6, Tiphareth, which means 'beauty', is associated with the sun and is also known as the Son or the Mediating Influence. The colour of the sphere is yellow, referring to the sun, and the image which is its symbol is that of a god sacrificed. All these attributes are those which the Christians specifically associate with Christ.

Now Tiphareth forms a triad with two opposites in spheres No. 4 and No. 5, Chesed ('mercy') and Geburah ('severity'), and we may take this triad as representing the active creation principles. We might expect that the remaining four spheres would represent the four elements, but in the symbolism of the Tree, fully-developed matter is not reached until we arrive at No. 10, Malkuth ('kingdom'), which betrays its materiality by being divided into four quarters coloured to represent the elements.

Instead, the system of ternaries extends all the way down the Tree. Tiphareth again forms part of the next triad with spheres Nos. 7 and 8, Netzach ('victory') and Hod ('splendour'), which are the spheres of

INVOLUTION AND EVOLUTION

Venus and Mercury. This triad may be considered as a reflection of the creative principles into the area of reproduction, the male and female principles inherent in the multiplication of living matter, mediated and energised through the self-generating principle of the sun.

This triad has another reflection in the spheres Nos. 7, 8 and 9, the last being Yesod ('foundation'), the sphere of the moon, seen here as the prototype of the *form* of physical matter. This last triad is immediately responsible for the appearance of the material in Malkuth at the bottom of the Tree.

So in its pattern, the Tree of Life shows creation in four descending stages, each triad being a reflection of the one above it in a strict progression from the Undifferentiated to the concrete.

The colours of the spheres, however, suggest a simpler view, based on the mixing of primary pigments discussed in an earlier chapter.

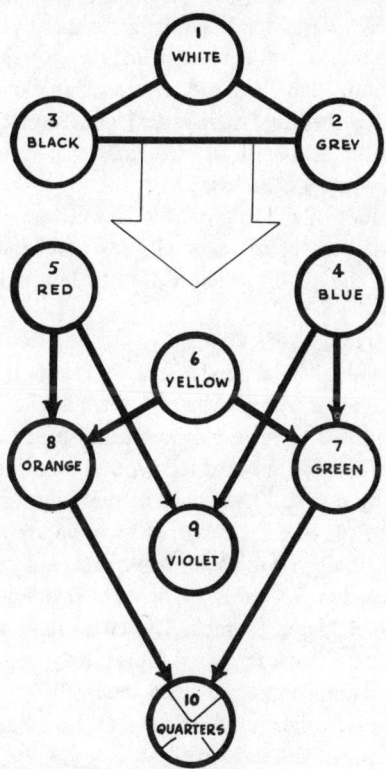

The triad 1, 2, 3 has, as we have said, no colour and, hence, does not take any direct part in creation. Spheres 4, 5 and 6 are the primary colours and are therefore equivalent to the original principles of creation. Sphere 7 is green, the mixture of the blue of 4, directly above it, and the yellow of the central sphere, 6. Orange is the colour of 8 and this is a mixture of the colours of 5, directly above it, and the central yellow. The lower central sphere, 9, is violet, the mixture of the two upper primary colours. The colouring of 10 may then be taken to be what we previously referred to as brown, the mixture of all three primary colours. When looked at in this way, the septenary follows its familiar pattern.

The arrangement of the paths between the spheres is intended to show that each of these patterns is equally valid and so are many others. Perhaps intentionally, the Tree of Life is an immensely complicated symbol, which has provided (and still provides) material for reflection for a great number of people. In a slight reference such as this, we cannot even skim the surface of the correspondences and significances read into the Tree by different individuals at different times. It is used as a medium of mystical contemplation, of magical ritual, of cosmological explanation, of divination and of psychological classification, among many other uses.

Although a product of predominantly Jewish thought, it is not, by any means, the exclusive preserve of the Jews and the pattern of the Tree itself combines the sacred symbols of both Jew and Christian.

The Tarot

Closely connected with the Cabalistic Tree of Life is the pack of cards used for divination by gypsies and others, known as the Tarot.

The Tarot is supposed to have originated in Europe during the 14th century and there is little doubt that its symbolism and that of the Tree of Life have a common origin. Although it resembles in many respects the ordinary pack of playing cards with which we are familiar, there is no record of its ever having been used for playing card games.

A complete pack has 78 cards, which are divided into two main groups, the Minor and Major Trumps. The latter have no suits, but the former, consisting of 56 cards, have four suits, Sceptres, or Wands, Cups, Swords and Pentacles, equivalent respectively to our modern Clubs, Hearts, Spades and Diamonds. Each suit has 14 cards, viz. Ace to Ten and King, Queen, Knight and Page.

INVOLUTION AND EVOLUTION

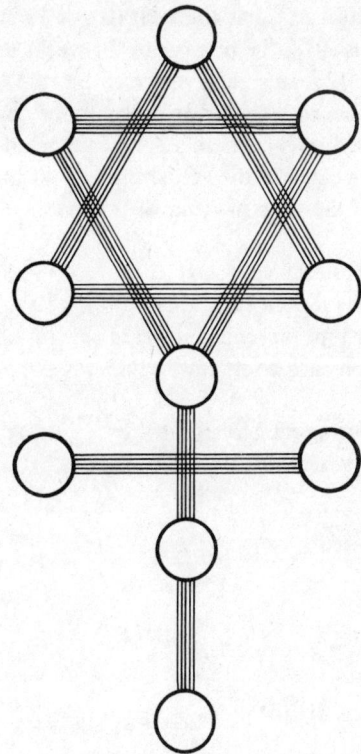

The Major Trumps consist of 22 cards, each of which has a name and a number. The name refers to a highly allegorical illustration appearing on the face of each card. One point of contact between the Tarot and the Tree of Life is that each of the Major Trumps is supposed to illustrate one of the paths between the spheres on the Tree.

Like the Zodiac, the Major Trumps of the Tarot provide a sequence illustrating the evolution of the human soul. The cards are numbered from 0 to 21, which shows that they are intended to be read as three septenaries plus one card, which stands apart from the rest. The Minor Trumps consist of four double septenaries in which each of the four suits represents one of the elements, while the cards of each suit repeat the symbols of the septenary in polarised form, one card representing the positive and one the negative aspect of each idea.

The ordinary modern pack of playing cards, while retaining a little of the symbolism of the Tarot, has altered it to a more mundane level. The number of the cards is 52,, the number of the weeks in the year, divided into four suits of 13 cards each, representing the four seasons. The Joker is the 'odd man out' needed to make up the complete year (since 52 weeks is only 364 days). There are 12 court cards to represent the 12 months of the year and the actual pips on all the cards should be equal to the days of the year, made up as follows:

```
55 'face' pips in each suit ........................220
26 small corner pips in each suit .................. 104
2 large corner pips on each court card ............. 24
1 centre-pip on each court card ................... 12
                                                    ___
Total representing the basic year .................360
Joker pips representing intercalary days ............  5
                                                    ___
                                                    365
```

8

Manifestations, Symbols and Practical Uses of the Number Seven

It is often difficult to sort out which occurrences of the number seven are the result of its being the sacred number and which, occurring naturally, are just prominent enough to act as psychological reinforcements of an existing prejudice towards the number.

Arithmetically, it is an 'awkward' number to use and children always seem to find particular difficulty in learning the seven-times table. In reckoning, adults frequently stumble over the answer to eight times seven. It is the only single-figure number for which there is no easy rule to find out whether it is a factor of a given number. Thus, a number is divisible by 2 if its last figure is even, by 3 if its digits, when added together, are divisible by 3, by 4 when its last two digits are so divisible, by 5 when its ends in 0 or 5, by 6 when it is divisible by 3 and is even, by 8 when its third last figure is even and its last two figures are divisible by 8 or when its third last figure is odd and its last two figures are divisible by 4 but not by 8, and by 9 when the sum of its digits reduces to 9. For 7, there is no such rule.

It has a peculiarity which may or may not have been known to the ancients in that, if any whole number which is not an exact multiple of 7, is divided by 7, the same sequence of figures appears in the answer as a recurring decimal, but the sequence starts at different points. Thus:

    1 divided by 7 is .$\overline{142857}$
    2 divided by 7 is .2857$\overline{142857}$
    3 divided by 7 is .42857$\overline{142857}$
    4 divided by 7 is .57$\overline{142857}$
    5 divided by 7 is .7$\overline{142857}$
    6 divided by 7 is .857$\overline{142857}$

Nevertheless, it can be assumed that it was not only the philosophers who spent a lot of time thinking about the sacred number. The mathematicians and calculators must also have played about with it to find out in what way it was different from other numbers.

The Rhind Mathematical Papyrus, an ancient Egyptian document written about 1650 BC and now in the British Museum, contains the following problem:

Problem 79 – Sum the geometrical progression of five terms, of which the first term is 7 and the multiplier 7.

The sum according to the rule. Multiply 2801 by 7.

1	2801
2	5602
4	11204
Total	19607

The sum by addition

Houses	7
Cats	49
Mice	343
Spelt	2401
Hekat	16807
Total	19607

The first thing we notice about this problem is the simple algorithm for multiplication by 7. It can be stated thus: Take the number to be multiplied; double it; double it again and add the three numbers together. This algorithm is based on the principles of binary arithmetic, i.e. arithmetic to the base 2, as used in most modern computers. In this system, there are only two figures, 1 and 0, from which all numbers are made up. Whereas, in the decimal system, the place values of the figures from right to left represent increasing powers of 10, in the binary system, they represent increasing powers of 2. The first eight binary

MANIFESTATIONS, SYMBOLS AND PRACTICAL USES

numbers, with their decimal equivalents are:

BINARY	DECIMAL
1	1
10	2
11	3
100	4
101	5
110	6
111	7
1000	8

We see that the number 7 is represented by the binary number 111, which means 2^2 plus 2^1 plus 2^0 or 4 plus 2 plus 1.

So far, there is no difficulty, but, in view of the stated aim of the Egyptian problem, it is a pity that the scribe has omitted to state how he arrived at the number 2801 with which he starts his multiplication. If his method is to be an effective substitute for the 'sum by addition' shown in the second part, we must presume that he knew of a simple and quick method for arriving at the number 2801, or rather the numbers which, when multiplied by 7, give the sums of any series of powers of 7 starting from the first power.

The ancient Egyptians had an additional need to be familiar with the workings of the number 7 in dealing with small measurements, because their next smaller unit of linear measure after the cubit was the palm, and seven palms made one cubit. So we find in the Rhind Papyrus many examples of problems involving division by 7. For example:

Problem 24 – A quantity plus one seventh of itself becomes 19. What is the quantity?

The Egyptians, unlike the Babylonians, had no way of representing decimal fractions and, in fact, only recognised two kinds of vulgar fractions, those whose numerator was 1 and those whose numerator was 1 less than the denominator. Thus, they would recognise as fractions 1/3, 1/7 or 1/226 and also 2/3 or 3/4, but a fraction such as 33/47 would be meaningless to them. So their method of dealing with fractions other than the 'recognised' ones becomes very complicated.

One and five eighths, for instance, had to be written as one plus one half plus one eighth, while one and eight fifteenths would be written as one plus one third plus one fifth.

For this reason, the ancient Egyptian would be quite unable to cope with our method of solving the problem quoted above:

$$x + \frac{x}{7} = 19$$

$$\frac{8x}{7} = 19$$

$$x = \frac{19 \times 7}{8} = 16 \tfrac{5}{8}$$

Instead, the Egyptian reasons thus: Consider the whole to be in seven parts; then one seventh added to it becomes eight. As many times as 8 must be multiplied to give 19, so many times must 7 be multiplied to give the required number.

He now proceeds to multiply 8 by whole numbers and simple fractions, adding the results together.

$$2 \,(\times 8 =) \quad 16$$
$$\tfrac{1}{4} \,(\times 8 =) \quad 2$$
$$\tfrac{1}{8} \,(\times 8 =) \quad 1$$

TOTAL $\quad 2 + \tfrac{1}{4} + \tfrac{1}{8} \quad 19$

Now, he multiplies the quantity $2 + \tfrac{1}{4} + \tfrac{1}{8}$ ($2\tfrac{3}{8}$) by 7

$$1 \quad - \quad 2 + \tfrac{1}{4} + \tfrac{1}{8}$$
$$2 \quad - \quad 4 + \tfrac{1}{2} + \tfrac{1}{4}$$
$$4 \quad - \quad 9 + \tfrac{1}{2}$$

TOTAL $\quad 7 \quad - \quad 16 + \tfrac{1}{2} + \tfrac{1}{8} \quad$ (i.e. $16\tfrac{5}{8}$)

Finally, he proves his result to be correct.

$$1 \quad - \quad 16 + \tfrac{1}{2} + \tfrac{1}{8}$$
$$\tfrac{1}{7} \quad - \quad 2 + \tfrac{1}{4} + \tfrac{1}{8}$$

TOTAL $\quad 1\tfrac{1}{7} - \quad 19$

MANIFESTATIONS, SYMBOLS AND PRACTICAL USES

Stellar Configurations

The mathematical problems quoted fall definitely into the category of conscious manipulations with the number seven. Into the opposite category of naturally-occurring phenomena which reinforce the status of the number must go the stellar configurations.

Three constellations have always been particularly prominent in man's view of the heavens, partly because of the brightness of their stars and partly because of their positions. They are the bright north circum-polar group, the Great Bear, the south circum-polar group, the Southern Cross, and the most prominent constellation on the celestial equator, Orion. The first-named is used as a pointer to the north pole star; the second, together with the very bright pair, Alpha and Beta Centauris, is used to find the position of the south celestial pole and the last is used, by the time of its rising, as a marker of the seasons. Now it is quite coincidental that the bright stars in each of these groups number seven.

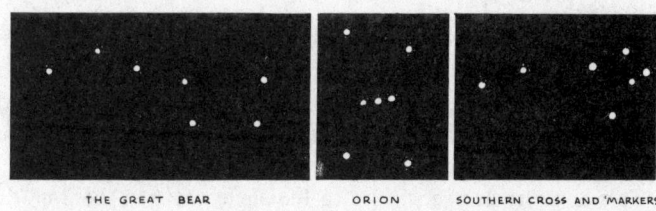

THE GREAT BEAR   ORION   SOUTHERN CROSS AND 'MARKERS'

Conversely, and therefore falling into the 'manipulated' category, the cluster of not-so-bright stars known as the Pleiades has had the number seven attached to it (as the seven sisters) from ancient times when, in fact, only six of the stars in the cluster are visible to the naked eye. The constellation figured prominently in the imagery of both the Hebrews and the Hindus as a septenary symbol.

The Pyramids

The basic symbolism of the pyramidal form has already been referred to. It is, of course, easy to apply symbolic explanations in retrospect, but the question which always intrudes itself is: Did the originators of the symbol see it in the same way? For instance, we can be positive in stating that the pyramid-builders of ancient Egypt saw the pyramid as a sun symbol, but did they also connect it with the septenary as we have done?

To try to answer this, let us take a particular pyramid rather than its idealised form and see what clues were built into it. We use the Great Pyramid of Cheops not because of any supposed extra esoteric significance attached to it as compared with the others, but because it has been examined and measured more often and with greater accuracy than any of the others.

The first thing which should be noted is that, if unit value is given to the length of one side of the base of a pyramid, the relative measurement of every other part can be determined if we know just one angle, that of the slope of the sides.

The angle at which the sides of the Great Pyramid slope, i.e. the angle between a side and the ground, is $51° 52'$. From this, we can immediately determine that the height of the pyramid is .6369 times the length of the base, while the length of a sloping edge is .9516 times the length of the base. We can also determine all the other angles, all the relative areas and the total volume without making another measurement.

Particular significance will therefore be attached to the angle of slope of the sides and it is surely not accidental that almost all known pyramids are constructed with a slope which is within a fraction of a degree of that of the Great Pyramid, and this slope is within 25 minutes of arc of *the angle which is one seventh of a complete circle*, $51° 25' 43''$. This angle is also very close to the angle between the 3-unit and 5-unit sides of a 3–4–5 triangle, the value in this case being $53° 8'$. The error of more than a degree is, however, far greater than the known errors in the construction as a whole.

Edwards has suggested in *The Pyramids of Egypt* that this slope results if the height of the pyramid is made to correspond with the radius of a circle the circumference of which is equal to the perimeter of the base of the pyramid. The angle derived from this relationship, $51° 51'$, is almost exactly the actual slope of the Great Pyramid. If this is deliberate – and it is difficult to see how it can be other than deliberate – it may still be a way of drawing attention to the fact that 'squaring the circle' in this way produces an angle which is almost exactly one seventh of a circle.

A more directly-symbolic septenary is exhibited in the internal structure of the Great Pyramid. Three chambers were constructed which, by their positions, can be taken to represent the three 'vertical' divisions of ancient cosmogeny, the heaven, earth and underworld, since the one, the so-called King's Chamber, is high in the structure,

MANIFESTATIONS, SYMBOLS AND PRACTICAL USES

while the Queen's Chamber is comparatively low in the structure and the third chamber is actually some distance below ground level. Connecting these chambers to the entrance of the pyramid is a system of passages which, like the river of Eden, begins as one and splits into four. Egyptologists usually interpret the structure as being the result of three changes of plan which took place during work on the pyramid and cite as evidence the fact that certain passages were bored through the stones after part of the building had been completed. In a sacred structure as carefully planned and as massive as the Great Pyramid, such wanton changes of heart seem out of character. If the building was planned in its present form, the 3 plus 4 septenary exhibited by its internal structure must also have been deliberate.

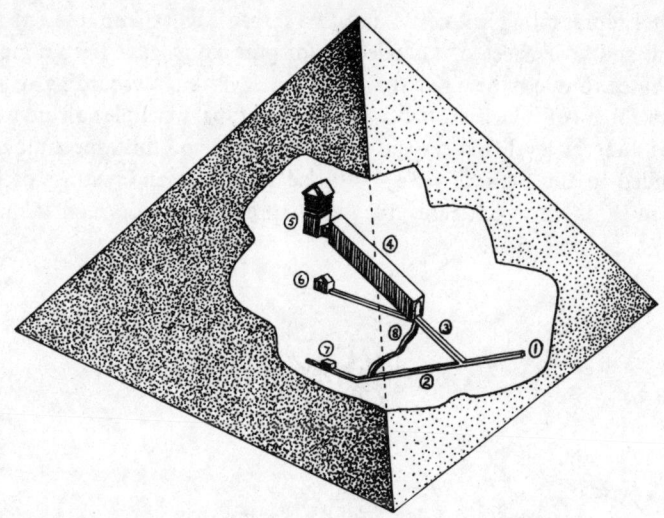

The internal structure of the Great Pyramid. 1 – the entrance to the downward passage. 2 – the downward passage continues below the level of the bedrock on which the pyramid is built. 3 – the upward passage leading to: 4 – the Grand Gallery. 5 – the King's Chamber. 6 – the Queen's Chamber. 7 – the small underground chamber. 8 – the 'odd man out' of the four subsidiary passages is this passage which runs almost vertically from the upward to the downward passage.

The Symbol of the Caduceus

The caduceus is one of the most ancient symbols used by man. Still in use today as a medical symbol, it has been found in exactly the same form as its modern usage on an early Sumerian cup dated about 2600 BC.

It consists of two serpents twined in opposite directions round a wand or staff, and its primary significance is obviously threefold. We may suggest that the two serpents represent two opposing principles while the wand represents the third, or reconciling, principle.

In the Sumerian version, the serpents have seven 'crossings', including the base, where the two tails are wrapped around each other, and the top, where the two heads face each other, the extended tongues almost touching.

There may be a connection here with the biblical story of the serpent and the Tree of Knowledge of Good and Evil. The Tree, in this case, is the equivalent of the wand, which may also be seen as a phallic symbol representing sexuality. The two serpents will then represent the 'good' and 'evil' faces of knowledge, for pure knowledge has no moral attributes, but can be used for 'good' or 'evil' ends according to the desire force (of which sexuality is the archetypal example) of the user.

At another level, the serpent stands for time and this aspect may be intended in the Sumerian case, stressed by the seven crossings of the two serpents, in which case, the wand represents eternity and the idea

The caduceus reproduced from the ancient Sumerian cup.

MANIFESTATIONS, SYMBOLS AND PRACTICAL USES

of the whole symbol is that time and eternity are not quantitative variations of the same basic principle, but are different in a qualitative sense, although the two are interwoven. The 'eternal Now' is suggested if the wand is taken to stand for the present with the snakes representing the past and future.

Even in the era which produced the Sumerian example, there was considerable contact between the cultures of India and Mesopotamia and it is possible that an entirely different idea was intended, for very ancient examples of the caduceus have been found engraved on stone in India. This idea involves another septenary connected with the human body, the seven *chakras*, centres or ganglia which are said to be successively awakened by a yogi through the raising of the *kundalini*, or fiery *serpent-power* which the hatha yogis claim lies coiled at the base of the spine. It must be understood that, while these ideas are expressed in anatomical terms, the yogis understand this to be the anatomy of a 'subtle body', coincident, but not identical, with the physical body.

The yoga adept maintains that, when a man breathes, it is not only air which enters his body, but also a vital force called *prana*, which, properly used and controlled, has the power to heal, revitalise and even change completely both the man's body and his consciousness. Through *prana*, currents are created in two subtle nerves in the spinal column, between which is a tube-like structure. This tube and the two nerves meet and pass through seven *chakras* located at various points on the spinal column, the highest of which is visualised as being situated above the physical head. The effect of certain yoga exercises, combining special breathing and mental concentration, is to arouse the serpent power and make it rise up the tube, impelled by the currents in the two nerves, until it passes into each of the *chakras* in turn, awakening a new form of consciousness in each. When it finally arrives at the highest *chakra*, complete illumination is given to the yogi and he attains to all knowledge.

There is a direct correspondence in this with the seven heavens of the Mohammedans; the awakening of the seventh *chakra* is exactly equivalent to entry into the seventh heaven.

It is highly significant that the *kundalini* is referred to as the 'serpent-power' by the yogis, for this makes the Sumerian caduceus an almost perfect representation of the arousal of this force, which passes through each *chakra* (shown as a crossing) until it arrives at the highest, above the head.

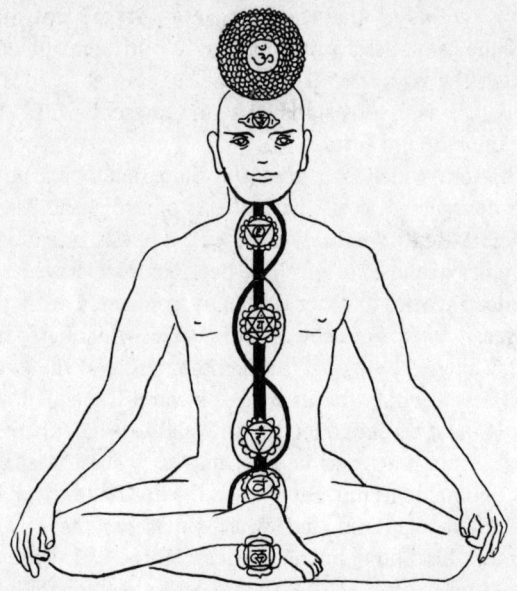

The seven chakras according to the traditions of hatha yoga.

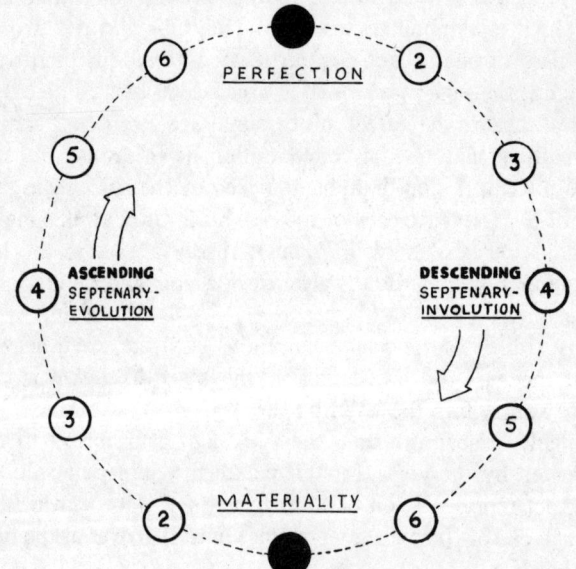

MANIFESTATIONS, SYMBOLS AND PRACTICAL USES

This process, according to yoga tradition, is the return of man to his original state of perfection. Creation, or the fall into the illusion of matter, is the reverse process and, by analogy, creation involves seven steps. Now the top and bottom steps are common to both the descent into matter, which is the action of creation or involution according to the point of view, and the return to perfection, for the one step is complete materiality and the other complete perfection. Between these two extremes are five descending and five ascending steps and the whole may be represented in circular form.

Thus the two septenaries resolve themselves into the 12 'houses' of the Zodiac and are the final justification for the 12-part division of the Wheel of Life. On this reading, Pisces represents the Ultimate Perfection as well as the primeval Void, while Virgo represents the ultimate 'illusion' of matter as well as the power needed to enable man to return to his Source.

The Seven-branched Candelabra

The seven-branched candelabra of the Hebrews refers, of course, to the prototype of this symbol in the original temple of Solomon. A lighted candle is symbolic of individual consciousness, as opposed to the light of the sun, which symbolises universal consciousness. The candelabra therefore refers to more than the simple idea of the seven days of creation; it is rather the symbol of the impact of the laws of creation upon the individual. Thus the central light, considered as being at rest in relation to the six 'planetary' lights (their planetary character is shown by the circular form of the branches), signifies the Jew's consciousness of God. 'Be still, and know that I am God' is the injunction which gives the reason for human rest from labour on the Sabbath.

The arrangement of the outer six lights is highly interesting in its numerical symbolism, for it shows directly (in a race which appears to reject the idea of the Trinity) that the effects of the three principles of creation are polarised in man, since each pair of lights occupies opposite ends of one of the three semi-circular branches. This means, for instance, that the outgoing principle can manifest as sociability on the one hand or aggressiveness on the other, while the reconciling principle can be seen in both firmness and vacillation. The only place where polarisation does not appear is at the Centre. The ethical implications of the implied doctrine are enormous and it is likely that the priestly

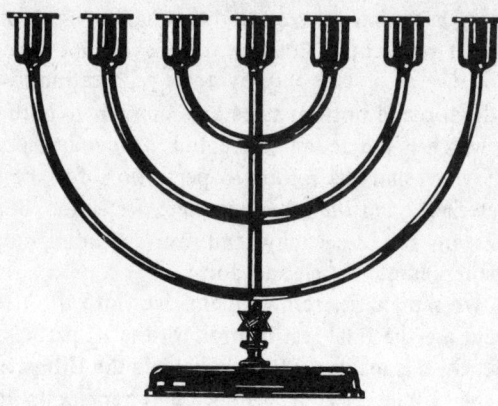

classes considered such teachings too dangerous for the masses. The symbol was, however, there for all who had the eyes to see and interpret it correctly.

Sex and Numerical Symbolism

It has often been said that, to Freud, all symbols had a sexual significance. Now, while agreeing that this is an overstatement and oversimplification of the facts, we must accept that he did tend to see sexuality in most symbols occurring in dreams. This does not necessarily mean that Freud saw man as a creature motivated entirely by sexual impulses. What he did see clearly was that there are sexual *correspondences* with almost every situation which is capable of affecting the psyche of man and that the interpretation of symbolic situations from dream experience in terms of sex gave a ready key to the force and direction of the emotions involved. And, after all, Freud was not alone in this notion; some of the world's best-known religious mystics have not hesitated to describe their ecstatic experiences of union with the divine in erotic terms — and in their case, we are dealing with the most lofty flights to which the human psyche can aspire.

The reason for such correspondences is not hard to find. The sexual experience involves the whole man. The man does not exist whose body can be occupied with lovemaking while his mind is busy proving the theorem of Pythagoras. All the senses, the intelligent mind, the emotional forces and the very spirit of the man are concentrated in the act, at the highest point of which a force greater than himself appears to take over and, for a brief moment, he is as helplessly in its power as a feather blown in a hurricane. Every orgasm is an initiation in miniature and appears to the participant like a rebirth.

Hence, says Freud, anything which is capable of shaking the psyche to its depths has its ready-made symbol in the sexual act and, in its effects on the man, it is indistinguishable from its sexual counterpart.

Folklore, and especially folk-magic, makes full use of this symbolic equivalence. As Frazer pointed out, there are still areas in rural Europe where, when the seed is in the ground, the farmer and his wife lie together in the fields and thereby identify themselves with the germinating seeds in order to encourage fertility.

We should expect that, since sexuality is an archetypal form of creation, its symbols would follow the familiar septenary pattern, thus showing the correspondence between the macrocosmic and microcosmic creation processes. Let us see if this is so.

The division of the sexes is, of course, the prime example of polarity. The primeval appearance of the opposites in the One is often symbolised as the separation of the male and female principles. This illustrates at once the idea of the ternary of creation, for the appearance of the male and female immediately involves the third principle or force, the mutual attraction between them. This is so self-evident that no explanation is called for, but the interesting part of the analogy is that it shows the impulse to return to the Source to be present even in the moment of creation, for this return is the reconciliation of the opposites as a result of their mutual attraction.

The most elegantly simple visual symbol of the polarity of creation in its sexual aspect is the *Yang-Yin* symbol of the Chinese. While at first glance this is a purely binary symbol, a little thought will show that, had this been the intention, the circle would simply have been divided into two halves by its diameter thus.

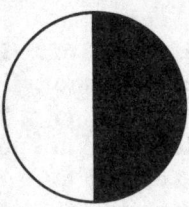

The curve which is actually used shows the presence of the third principle, resulting in both penetration and withdrawal shown by the inward and outward bulges.

If this symbol is properly drawn, it is based on the construction shown below:

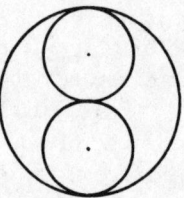

In this construction, the two inner circles have half the radius of that of the outer circle and, since the area of a circle is proportional to the square of its radius, the large circle is divided into four equal areas. So the fourfold division of manifestation is inherent in the threefold symbol of creation and the *Yang-Yin* symbol conveys the complete 3—4 septenary in one simple figure.

Part of the force of the sexual image is that all objects, principles and ideas are capable of being classified as masculine or feminine according to their characteristics. Some of these classifications are shown below.

MASCULINE		FEMININE
Elongated	as opposed to	Round or Hollow
Angular	as opposed to	Curved
Active	as opposed to	Passive
Outgoing	as opposed to	Withdrawing
Hard	as opposed to	Soft
Strong	as opposed to	Weak
Vertical	as opposed to	Horizontal
Solar	as opposed to	Lunar
Stable	as opposed to	Variable
Positive	as opposed to	Negative

These characteristics are given as a set of opposites, but most sexual classifications are relative. Thus the strong man is masculine in relation to the weak, but is himself feminine in relation to the divine. There is, in this sense, a continuous spectrum of sex rather than a clear-cut division. This is true in human sexuality, for every man contains within himself feminine characteristics in greater or lesser degree and every woman contains some masculine characteristics. In the middle of the scale stands the hermaphrodite, half male and half female, who symbolises the reconciliation of the opposites and points the way of the evolutionary return to the Source. For this reason, Mercury, the messenger and arbiter of the gods is often considered as a hermaphrodite; he carries the caduceus and the sphere of his own activity is hidden wisdom; his planet is closest to the sun.

Many sexual symbols are ambivalent in character. As a biblical personage, Salome represents an evil image of femininity, using her power to inflame desire in those who watch her erotic dance, to obtain the head of John the Baptist. Traditionally, hers is the dance of the seven veils, in which each diaphanous covering is removed in turn, showing more and more clearly the figure beneath, until she dances completely naked. On the face of it, this dance is the systematic arousal of lust during which the watcher becomes the dancer's slave through desire, but the dance of the seven veils is also the symbol of the evolutionary return to Perfection, the desire for which is implanted in man as surely as is his own sexuality and, like sexual desire, it grows stronger and stronger the closer man approaches his Goal. At the final stage, he enters into the *conjunctio oppositorum*, symbolised again by sexual union.

Nudity is thus a symbol both of the innocence of beginning (the state before the 'fall' into materiality – e.g. Adam in the Garden of Eden) and of the ultimate Perfection to which man must return in the end. Artists of all times have apprehended the force of this symbol and have used the erotic as a vision of the Perfect.

Pythagorean number symbology stresses the sexual attributes of the integers. One, and all odd numbers, are masculine, while two, and all even numbers, are feminine. This association is, in part, determined by the shapes exhibited by numbers when they are represented by dots. All even numbers divide into two parts with a hole in the middle, while a similar division of the odd numbers results in a central unit. Thus the symbolism is crudely phallic and, in fact, the number three is taken as the representative of the male genitals.

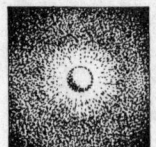 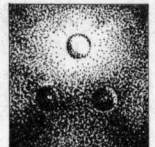 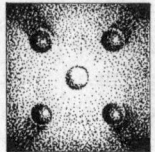 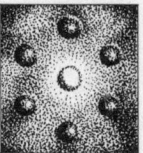

THE ODD (MASCULINE) NUMBERS

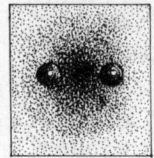 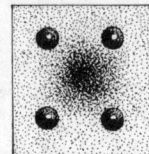 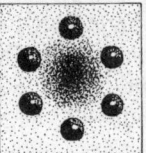 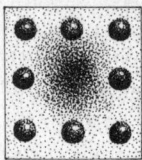

THE EVEN (FEMININE) NUMBERS

The Pythagorean proof of the dominance of masculinity is simple; if an odd number is added to an even number, the result is always an odd number. This precept can, of course, be seen as a piece of blatant sophistry in which the wish is father to the thought (Pythagoras' world was a man's world), for it is easy to counter by pointing out that if two odd numbers or two even numbers are added together, the result is always an even number, similarly when an odd and an even number are multiplied together, suggesting that *femininity* is dominant. All of which goes to show that it is fatally easy to play around with number symbolism to make it agree with preconceived ideas.

Woman exists in one of three states; the virgin, the lover and the mother. The abstract image of womanhood includes all three aspects and they are often embraced in the image of a goddess, although logically they are mutually exclusive. They are definitely interwoven in the archetypal image of woman in the subconscious which Jung has named the *anima* and which is really the feminine side of a man's nature, personified and provided with a sort of autonomous life by the man himself. This is the image against which he unconsciously compares the real women in his life and which, projected on to one woman, makes him feel that he has found a true soul-mate, sometimes with disastrous results, for this kind of love is really directed towards a part of the self and it is as blind to reality as the proverb suggests.

A man's real mother is likely to provide the first experience man has of woman and so the mother-image is the foundation of the *anima*. Gradually, under the influence of his growing sexuality, the mother-image is overlaid by the characteristics of the lover and so becomes the image of an object of sexual desire, creating vaguely-discerned yearnings in the adolescent and forming the core of the sexual phantasies of the young man. Then, as he gains experience of womankind, a new concept is added to the previous two, the romantic idea of virginity. Thus the archetype becomes a whole, the temporal order of the expected sequence of virgin, lover and mother having been reversed in the process. So the creation of the *anima* involves three principles similar in form to the divine principles of creation, for the virgin and mother are opposites and the lover is the intermediary between the two.

In a similar way, the first feminine deity to be acknowledged by man is the Great Mother, usually identified with the earth, and a symbol of protection and fertility. All that has life is believed to come from the womb of Mother Earth, including the human race. The worship of the Great Mother is a common characteristic of the matriarchal society, in which the status of the male is secondary. As the pendulum begins to swing and the male takes over the dominant role, the goddess becomes transformed into the ruler of love; the erotic overlays, but does not entirely replace, the maternal. This is the image represented by Astarte and Venus. The worship of the goddess is now likely to be orgiastic without necessarily including rites to promote fertility. Lastly, there emerges the lofty notion of the virgin-goddess, who is often the virgin-mother of the chief god.

The symbolic idea of virginity needs some examination, for we have been conditioned to equate the virgin with innocence, which is a false equation. As a divine symbol, the virgin represents the end of the downward path of involution and the real beginning of evolution. This is a moment of rebirth; the spirit is, as it were, born from the perfected flesh to begin its journey home. It is virginal simply because it is newly-orientated towards its Source, not because it is innocent of 'evil', of lust, the craving for power or any other negative trait, for all these have been experienced during the involutionary journey. Laden with 'sin' it may be, but the spirit has been aroused and the process of return begins. This is why Virgo is placed at the very bottom of the Wheel of Life.

While we have been dwelling on the threefold aspect of woman, we must not forget that the viewpoint is that of the *male*. It is the *anima* in a *man* which is being described and the goddess' worshippers are *men*.

The subconscious influence of this archetypal image on the man himself is profound. The 'woman within' often impels him to a course of action which seems completely foreign to his overt personality, so that, afterwards, he is likely to say 'I don't know what made me do it.' The *anima* is the repository of a large body of ideas and impulses which the man has at some time or other repressed because they do not fit in with his self-image. Consciously, he has forgotten that these impulses ever existed, yet they are there, constantly awaiting the opportunity to express themselves.

The *anima* has a very large influence on the psychological type of the man and is certainly reflected in the distinct psychological states which manifest themselves from time to time and which depend on the mixture of the mother, lover and virgin images, singly, two together or all three in proportion, analogous with the mixing of the primary colours.

As a crude illustration of how this creative energy works, we imagine a man whose *anima* is dominated by the maternal and virginal images. This man will be unconsciously seeking a 'spiritual mother'. Idealised, she will be someone upon whom he will feel entirely dependent for a lead in his own inner attitude to life. His sexual energy is likely to be sublimated in the search for 'higher' planes of contact and, when confronted by the reality of the woman upon whom he has projected impossible qualities, he is certain to feel lost and cheated. Such a man will tend to be very introverted and to withdraw from all frivolously gregarious activities. He is unlikely to be successful in business but may succeed in artistic activity if he has the continuous urging of a dominating woman to keep him at the right pitch.

Obviously over-simplified, this picture also leaves out of account all influences except that of the *anima*, but it does show the creative combination of two of the three principles of the *anima*. Our main purpose in drawing the picture is to show that the septenary of creation is a pattern which is universal in application and is not limited to the case of divine, *ab-initio* creation.

The Psychological Septenary

Symbols would have no significance if there were no intelligent beings to observe them. They derive their meaning partly from the reality they represent and partly from their psychological effects on the mind which contemplates them. A symbol cannot be said to exist as such until it has been recognised by the human mind and most people would go even further than this and say that it is the human mind which *creates* the symbol.

Certainly, man is fascinated by symbols and the more mysterious they are, the greater the fascination. It is not for nothing that the Riddle of the Sphinx has always been with us; not the ancient Greek riddle, but the universal one posed by the Great Sphinx of Giza. We recognise in this figure an enigma; we *know* the figure is symbolic; we *feel* its brooding emotional impact; we can *explain* the symbolic import of many of its elemental parts; but we cannot lay hold of the total inner meaning of the whole image. However we intellectualise about the Sphinx and relate it to what is known about the culture of which it was born, there remains a great mystery and the mystery itself is part of the symbol. Man loves to penetrate into the unknown, but if he once knows all that is to be known about what was previously veiled from him, he loses interest and goes away dissatisfied. A true symbol is significant at many levels so that 'explaining' one level of meaning only serves to reveal a deeper layer of mystery which again must be explained. It has been said that the penetration of *any* true symbol, if carried through all its levels, must eventually lead the mind to the Ultimate Source, the Creator, for Reality is One and only appears to be differentiated because we have not comprehended it fully.

Man, in this view, creates the symbols he uses, but he does so under the influence of the Reality which lies behind them and which draws him onwards. This is the standpoint of the mystic, for whom symbols are stepping-stones leading to his Goal, God. The psychologist, depending on the school to which he belongs, will describe the process differently, as one of self-realisation, integration or individuation. If he is a behaviourist, he will refuse to discuss the inner process itself, but will refer to its visible effects on the actions and attitudes of the individual, comparing these with certain systematic 'norms'. Even he, however, will recognise man's apparent need to explain himself to himself and to relate himself to the world around him, because he recognises in a man who is unable to do so a disorientation which is reflected in his reactions to the stimuli which impinge upon his life.

If we have tended to describe the significance of our central symbol, the septenary, in religious and philosophical terms almost exclusively, we must not forget that there are direct correspondences in pure psychology. It is not only a philosophical concept that the mind of man *creates* directly, but a psychological one as well. To Freud, for instance, 'psychic reality', which may be pure illusion from the point of view of an outsider, is every bit as valid for the mind which experiences it as is physical reality and produces exactly similar effects on the subconscious mind; in psychiatry, the two are virtually indistinguishable.

The division of ancient man's world into three regions: heaven, earth and underworld, has an exact parallel in the psychological division of the total man into super-conscious, conscious and sub-conscious, all three areas of the psyche being necessary to the creative activity of the mind, which then acts through the four 'elements' of sensation, rational thought, emotion and will.

Without necessarily involving ourselves in a dualistic psychology, we can say that man consists of essence and personality, the former referring to man-as-he-is and the latter to man-as-he-appears (*personna* – the mask used by a character in an ancient drama). Psychologists who belong to the behaviourist school adopt the view that only the latter aspect of man is capable of being studied objectively and that to look for causal relationships, which are impossible to demonstrate in terms of overt behaviour, is unscientific. Some mathematicians adopt a similar view about their own discipline, maintaining that their arguments are equally valid whether or not any 'meaning' can be attached to them to relate them to the 'real' world.

Both are right if they consider themselves limited by what can actually be demonstrated, but just as there is a philosophy of mathematics which goes beyond such limitations, there is a philosophy of psychology which looks for the essence behind the personality as revealed by human behaviour. Philosophy, in this sense, is bound to be somewhat speculative in appearance, whether it treats of the background to mathematics or psychology, for instead of starting with empirically-discovered 'facts' and working backwards to find generalised principles which account for them, it starts with postulates which are believed to be universal principles and shows by logical steps how these principles lead to the 'facts'. The speculative element is due to the fact that the original postulates can never be *proved* to be true. In using them, the philosopher is relying on a faculty which he considers to be superior to that of rational thought and which is usually referred to as *nous*.

Behavioural psychology is concerned only with the quaternary. It has discovered that personality types can be classified satisfactorily by reference to two dimensions or scales, let us say, the extraversion – introversion scale and the stability–instability scale. By laying out these two scales on axes at right angles to each other, it is theoretically possible to pinpoint any personality on the resulting two-dimensional continuum and thus refer to it by the equivalent of Cartesian co-ordinates. The psychology of personality then becomes a matter of showing that a man who is placed at a certain point on the continuum will tend to react in a particular way to particular stimuli. Why this should be so is outside the terms of reference under which the behavioural psychologists work.

The psychological philosopher, however, will not be content to remain within the province of descriptive classification. He will explore the causative reality behind the appearance and will try to formulate the principles of the essence of man which account for his visible personality. This is the realm of the ternary. If we concede that the real man *creates* the visible personality, we are bound to accept that the microcosmic creative principles used by – or which constitute – the real man correspond in some way to the principles of the macrocosmic Creator and are therefore triune in character.

What distinguishes man from inert matter is his relationship with the rest of the cosmos. He *acts* towards the world, *reacts* to the stimuli which the world provides and is capable of *ordering* both his actions and reactions in a purposeful manner. The combination of these principles into a pattern of behaviour is the creation of a personality. If we consider man apart from the cosmos so as to isolate the essence which we are seeking, we can refer to the three principles as outgoing, incoming and ordering or, more generally, as the proceeding, returning and abiding principles.

To appreciate the necessity for these three principles, we must again try to imagine the state of no-thingness which precedes the crystallisation of a personality. Before anything can proceed out of nothing, the *principle* of proceeding must establish itself by polarisation, which automatically implies the establishment of its opposite, the principle of returning. On their own, however, these two principles cannot give rise to any form of structural relationship; a third, ordering, principle is called for to hold the others in equilibrium-without-annihilation, hence the abiding principle.

Man-in-essence is seen to be continuously evolving. He is not something static, but is always *becoming*. This is the principle of proceeding in operation. As he evolves, he finds within himself the urge to perfection, seeking always that which is 'higher' than his present state; but perfection is the state from which he arose and so we see that this urge is the returning principle in operation. The third, or abiding, principle is what maintains the individual in existence during his evolutionary journey. It is the principle of *being* as opposed to that of *becoming*. Its own tendency is to maintain the *status quo* in any situation and so it acts towards the realisation of what has already been attained rather than to urge the individual forward or backward. In analogy with the flow of time, it is equivalent to the present, the here and now, rather than the past (returning principle) or the future (proceeding principle).

This, then, is the ternary principle of the essence of man. How do these three principles manifest themselves in the personality? The proceeding and returning principles are held in approximate equilibrium by the third principle; only approximate, because personality is never completely static. The first two principles form the dimension from extraversion to introversion, while the degree of the abiding principle necessary to counterbalance the other two determines the position of the personality along the scale of the second dimension between stability and instability.

There is a difference of pattern here which troubles most people when they first face these ideas. On the one hand, we have two principles apparently being translated into two directions on a single scale of values, while, on the other hand, the third principle is translated into a single scale of values of its own. How can we reconcile this with the idea of the triangle of principles in which each of the three contributes equally to the whole? The answer lies in the way in which the three principles arise. The proceeding and returning principles, when viewed from the 'outside', are opposites. They could not exist together were their effect not balanced by the third principle. Now, because it is balancing the other two principles, there is no logical necessity to introduce an opposing principle in the third case. The 'opposite' of being should be non-being, but by definition, non-being is not a principle at all. In a slightly different sense, *either* the proceeding or returning principle may be considered as the 'opposite' of the abiding principle. Either a thing is static or it is in motion. It cannot be both at once. It is this very fact which enables us to see the three principles as a 'triangle of forces'.

If we now resolve the forces marked 'proceeding' and 'returning'

MANIFESTATIONS, SYMBOLS AND PRACTICAL USES 141

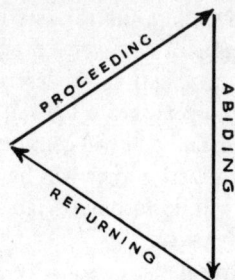

into components at right angles to and parallel with the force marked 'abiding', this is what we get:

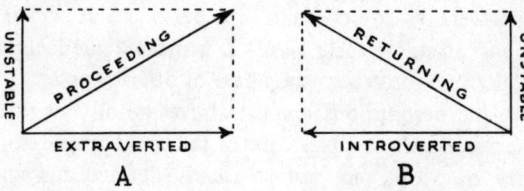

Now at A and B we have two arrows pointing upwards representing components which may be added together and which then balance the opposed 'abiding' force shown by the arrow at C. Let us call the direction of the two small arrows 'instability' and that of the large arrow 'stability'. We are now left with an arrow pointing right at A and an equal and opposite arrow at B. Call the former 'extraverted' and the latter 'introverted' and we have all the components needed to describe our 'personality-field' of four directions.

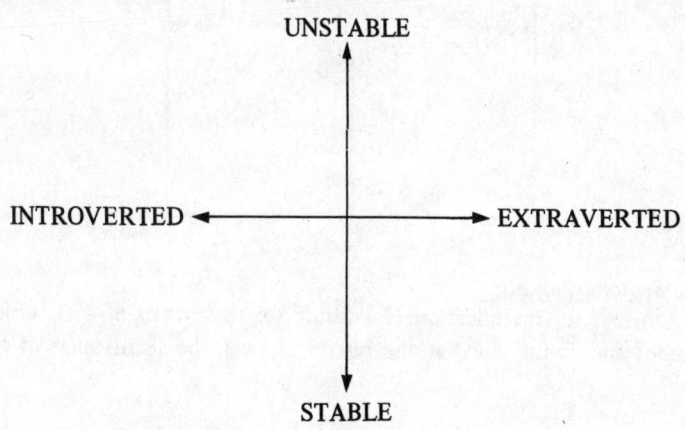

Now a personality placed in a 'north-easterly' direction on this map will have the greatest degree of extraversion and also of instability and it does not take much imagination to describe his reactions to the world. He is the type who gets into a fight at the drop of a hat. Just raise your eyebrows at him and you will get your nose punched.

Someone in the 'south-east' corner will have maximum stability as well as extraversion. He will uniformly sociable and gregarious and will be the 'life and soul' of any party.

The outstanding quality of the personality placed in the south-west corner will be his calmness in all circumstances. Independent of the need to be admired by others, he will nevertheless tend to be the rock to which others cling.

The north-west sector contains the personalities which are both withdrawn and unstable. The result is a morbid preoccupation with themselves, gloom, moroseness and a fear of other people.

Naturally, the descriptions applied above are all the extremes, the unlikely characters whose places are in the exact corners of the plan. The majority of people are not so clearly defined and will tend to cluster fairly close to the centre so that, statistically, the diagram will look like this:

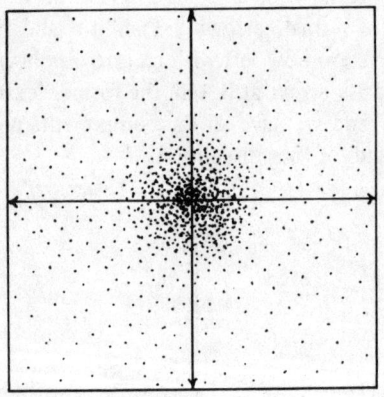

The Septenary of Man
We started our investigation as a search for the origins of a numerical symbol and found that, at the historical level, the significance of the

septenary was to be found in a world catastrophe, reinforced at the practical level by the discoveries of the astronomer-priests and, finally, explained by the philosophers as an inherent pattern of creation. It is not irrelevant to ask whether the correspondences revealed have any significance for the individual here and now. Does it really matter to us that creative activity is seen as conforming to a septenary pattern? In any case, how *real* is this conformation; is it just a pretty concept developed in the course of philosophical speculation upon an ancient symbol or does it correspond in some way with reality?

The answers we give to these questions will depend to a large extent on the way in which we should answer a much more basic question: What do I conceive to be the purpose of my existence? This is, of course, one of the fundamental problems of philosophy. At the same time, every dogmatic religious system is based on the supposition that *the answer to the question is known*. To ask the question at all, therefore, is to insert a big question mark after the dogmas on which blind faith is built. For this reason, it is not uncommon for the young man who has been reared in an atmosphere of strict orthodoxy and who meets systematic philosophy head-on for the first time in his university years, to swing, temporally at least, to the opposite pole of atheism or agnosticism. Often, however, the pendulum swings back after a time and the man finds himself re-embracing his original beliefs, but from a new standpoint, his philosophical thought having given him an insight into the meaning of the very dogmas it earlier caused him to reject out of hand.

The question itself, disarmingly simple in appearance, turns out, on analysis, to be complicated by the concepts it embodies. The central word is 'purpose' and this is a word which needs extremely careful handling. We talk about *the* purpose of existence as if purpose can exist on its own, but the word automatically implies an *author* of the purpose. Activity which is not controlled or directed by a conscious agency cannot be called purposeful activity. So if we ask about the purpose of existence, we must decide on whose behalf we are asking. Is it the individual's own purposes we are enquiring into or is the implied Author the actual Source of the existence whose purpose we wish to know?

If we are enquiring only into the purposes whose instigator is the individual himself, we need not look very far. Assuming the individual to create his own purpose, we are bound to answer that this is simply the pursuit of pleasure and the avoidance of pain. At this level, these twin purposes are quite sufficient and self-evident.

It is quite obvious that this is not what we mean by the question and we are really seeking a higher purpose. The atheist, if he is to be consistent, must answer that, from this point of view, life has *no* purpose because it has no conscious Cause. Then why, we may ask, do so many professed atheists lead highly moral lives; why do they not simply grab the pleasures which are available and avoid the unpleasant or arduous duties of life, the undertaking of which implies a higher order of existence than the purely personal?

If the question has any meaning, then, it can only be based on the Authorship of a Supreme Being, responsible for the creation and maintenance of the existence of the individual.

There is another assumption in this simple-sounding question which is difficult to tie down. I speak of 'my existence' as if it were a simple fact, but what is this 'I' to which I refer so glibly? I sit here at this desk with a pen in my hand making marks on a sheet of paper. How do I know that I am here? Because I am aware of the sensations of my body in relation to its surroundings. Note the words I have to use – *my* body and *its* surroundings. These things are not me; they are *objects* of my awareness. So I shut out the sensations and try to concentrate my awareness upon itself. A flood of images and ideas passes in review on my mental cinema screen. I am aware of these images and ideas, so they are also objects of my awareness and, therefore, not me. I turn off the flow of thoughts and images. What is left which I can call 'I'? Nothing which can be described, yet in that moment of supreme stillness when even the thought of self has vanished and no-thing remains, I still *am*. More than this I cannot say; whatever can be said is negative in form. In the stillness, there is no differentiation, no 'here and there', no 'then and now', no space, no time, no object of awareness.

The experiment which I have described can be repeated by any conscious individual and, if it is successful, must have the same result. What does this imply? It means that there is no way in which my 'I' can be distinguised from your 'I' or from any other 'I'. All are the same. *There is only one 'I'*. This is what we have referred to under the numerical symbol of the One. Is it any wonder that some of the world's greatest mystics have been accused of rank blasphemy when they have penetrated into this mystery at first hand and have experienced it as a

MANIFESTATIONS, SYMBOLS AND PRACTICAL USES

flash of Truth, exclaiming 'I and God are One!'? Yet the Bible itself speaks of God's own description of Himself as 'I AM THAT I AM'.

We may adopt the position that it is impossible for a mere man ever to know the purpose of his own existence, since this is known only to his Creator. But is this not itself an immediate pointer to the answer? Can we not at once deduce that the ultimate purpose of our existence is to come to a realisation of the Identity of the Self?

There is a Hindu myth which expresses this idea in an aesthetically-satisfying form. In the beginning, it says, the One existed alone, but because of Its own undifferentiated nature, It could not become aware of Itself. To remedy this, the only imperfection in the Perfect, It allowed Itself to manifest as the Many, each individual of which was unique and therefore saw the rest of manifestation from a different point of view, each believing that it was a separate self. Then, each individual was turned around to face its Source and, as it was drawn back into the One, it realised that it was itself the One. In this way, the One became aware of Itself through the Many and Perfection was restored.

On this view, evolution, seen as the ever-increasing awareness of Integrality, is both process and purpose. Becoming is a necessary part of Being or, to put it differently, Involution, Evolution and pure Being are the three inseparable principles of Selfhood. The Self, consequently, is *static* insofar as its essence is unchanging, *dynamic* insofar as it takes part in the total circular motion of evolution, *outward-facing* in relation to the rest of manifestation and *inward-facing* in relation to its Source.

This is the septenary of created Man, his Selfhood and his Purpose, the three principles of his creation resulting in the four 'elements' which describe his present situation.

9
From Phenomena to Philosophy

This quest for the origins of the 'magical' nature of the number seven has led us into some unexpected areas of thought. It has been necessary to look at the meaning of the number through the eyes of alchemy, astronomy, folklore, philosophy, religion and psychology and the contributing factors have been put together disjointedly. Let us now take a bird's eye view of the situation and try to draw the strings together into a coherent whole.

The one feature which, more than any other, distinguishes man from the 'lower' creatures is his consciousness of self-hood. He is aware of his own unity and, in his self-reflecting moments, he is *aware of his awareness*.

It is this which impels him to ask the question 'Why?' continuously from the cradle to the grave. On this single question, the whole of science and philosophy has been built. Why does it rain? Why do things fall to the ground? Why does the sun not fall to the ground? Why am I here?

When man asks 'Why?', he is searching for causes of phenomena, but behind each question is a more personal need; he wants to find a meaning and purpose in the universe as a whole, which will give meaning and purpose to his own existence. What he is really saying is, 'This entity which I call myself and which is so important to me, is it an accident in a purposeless world, or is it here for a reason?'

The very fact that he can ask the question shows that he knows that there is something which we call Truth *which already exists*, waiting to be found. This knowledge is part of being. Suppose he now denies that there is a purpose in life; then he must also deny that there is Truth, for one implies the other. At its most basic level, therefore, the question answers itself. The universe and life have a purpose, but a purpose implies an Author of the purpose, so what we call God is dialectically discovered in the existing knowledge of man.

There is, however, a barrier to the immediate discovery of ultimate Truth in this way. The closer we approach to Truth in discourse, the more abstract our arguments have to become until, at a certain point, we have to admit to ourselves that words are no longer competent to discuss the subject at all. We then tend to use symbols as signposts to what we are trying to realise. Words themselves are, of course, no more than symbols, each with a range of meanings which depend on the context. Many words are incapable of even circular definition, among them the word we have just been using so glibly — 'Truth'.

Philosophy then turns out to be, like mathematics, simply a method of manipulating symbols. Hopefully, the pattern which emerges bears some relationship to the truth which underlies it and which cannot adequately be expressed in words.

We have said that man *knows* that Truth is there, waiting for him to find it. Thus, some part of him *must be already in contact* with Truth or Reality. The suggestion here is that some part of man already knows the Truth, but he does not realise consciously that he knows. When he makes a new discovery, he recognises it as such only because it was there all the time. The recognition of a new fact invariably makes the discoverer exclaim, 'Of course, that's it!', as if he were remembering something long-forgotten.

Certain patterns of appearance strike a man as being meaningful because of his subconscious recognition of the parallel between appearance and Truth. In other words, it is not just a question of man searching for Truth, but equally of Truth thrusting itself into his thinking. This innate knowledge which man possesses is not a product of learning. It is present in the unschooled savage as well as in the Doctor of Science. The savage will have no ready means of rationalising his knowledge, but it will still show itself in the concepts he forms as a result of his experience of the world. And so he will attach to certain symbols a feeling of the numinous in the measure that their form and pattern correspond with his inner knowledge.

For this reason, symbols precede philosophy. No man sits down to think up a symbol (except, perhaps, an advertising man seeking a sales-image for a new detergent); we abstract symbols from the world around us because we recognise their significance subconsciously. Having isolated a symbol from its normal context, we start to rationalise it, or try to give it 'meaning' in a semantic sense. The real meaning of a symbol, however, has nothing to do with semantics; it was there when we first recognised the symbol and no amount of 'explaining' will add anything to it.

This is the case with the symbol of the septenary of creation. It was recognised by men who lived thousands of years before the Christian era, men whom we should be inclined to call 'primitive'. If they explained it to themselves, their explanations would almost certainly be very different from ours, but what are ours more than pointing out the correspondences between one symbol and another? Truth itself does not change, only our conscious perception of it. All we have been able to do here is to look at these varying perceptions in relation to our central symbol. The first of these perceptions is entirely subconscious and recognises no more than the pattern of a set of appearances in an awe-inspiring natural catastrophe.

It has to be accepted* that, at some stage in the early history of civilisation, a catastrophe of world-proportions took place, great enough to kill off a large part of the earth's flora and fauna, including humanity itself. Obviously, destruction was not complete and there were *some* survivors to tell the story. The cause of the catastrophe was a celestial body comparable in appearance to the two most prominent bodies now in our skies, the sun and moon. Let us suppose that one of the survivors were asked to tell the story of the events in which he had been involved. This might be the form of his account, which we have related by means of marginal notes to the relevant biblical stories:

(Garden of Eden)

> Once upon a time, the world was a beautiful garden in which men lived in contentment and which contained everything needed for their comfort. We cultivated the soil, tended our cattle and hunted the wild creatures for food and lived at peace with the gods and with our neighbours.
>
> But it came to pass that there arose certain evil men who, dissatisfied with their lot, began to covet the possessions of others. Some of their leaders learned the secrets of the gods and used them to increase their own power and goods.

*See Appendix 1.

And the gods looked down on them and said, 'These men who are evil think that they are gods. Let us destroy them before they learn the secrets of immortality itself. They shall be driven from the garden with the fiery sword and the evil men shall be destroyed by fire or drowned by the water which flows from the four rivers of the garden.'

(Sodom and Gomorrah)

So the gods sent for two of their number, the water-moon, who had, until then, peacefully regulated the tides of the sea, and the fire-moon, who had dwelt in a far corner of heaven and had not before been seen by mortal eyes.

And the chief of the gods, the sun, said to the two moons, 'Go now and destroy the earth, for its inhabitants have become evil. Do not rest until every evil thing has been wiped out, but if you find even one among them who is not evil, you shall allow him to escape your destruction.'

We first saw the fire-moon approaching when it was still far away and it looked like a bright star moving swiftly across the heavens. Some of us saw this as an omen and began to prepare ourselves for disaster, while others scoffed and said, 'What is that to me? How can this newcomer in the heavens presume to judge me, who am equal to the gods?'

But the fire-moon drew quickly near and, soon, it was as big as the water-moon. The waters of the ocean began to heave. Great tides swept into the land and we knew that judgment was at hand. We fled to the hills and sheltered in a cave with our women from the wrath to come. With my own eyes, I saw the beginning of the end. I stood on a mountain-top watching that huge globe in the sky and, even as I watched, it began to glow a fiery red. Then, it split itself in two halves. There was a great flash of red light and the one half of the god rent itself into a thousand pieces, which soon began to descend upon the earth in trails of fire. Each of the thousand pieces rained burning rocks upon the ground and the whole earth shook. Below me, I saw the forests catch fire and soon it seemed as if the whole world was alight. Nothing could live in the flames which swept the earth.

(The gods)

For many days, the land burned; the smoke from the fires reached almost to the stars and all that we had known was utterly destroyed. Now and then, we caught a glimpse through the smoke of the sun or the water-moon or the remaining half of the fire-moon, but most of the time we could not tell whether it was night or day. Great, thick clouds now covered the sky, mixed with the smoke, and the heavens opened and hail and rain came down the like of which had never been seen by man. Great winds roared through the fire so that even the rain had no effect upon it and it continued to burn in the midst of the water.

(The elements)

Then, the earth shook as though two worlds had come together and we were thrown to the ground, every man, woman and child who had hidden in the cave. There was a roaring and crashing and cracks opened up in the earth all around us.

(The flood)

But the most terrifying event was still to come. The gods were still not satisfied that all evil men had been destroyed and now they sent a wall of water over the land, which seemed to tower as high as the mountain tops. The whole earth disappeared under that great mass of water and we knew that the end had come. Unable to support the sight, I knew no more and it was as if I were dead.

When we again lifted our faces to the sky, we saw there a rainbow where the fire-moon had been. It was a sign of peace from the gods. We knew that the evil moon had plunged with its fire deep into the bowels of the earth and would never again seek to destroy man as long as he kept from waywardness. But, periodically, we heard its rumbling from beneath the earth and we felt the earth shake and saw the fire break out from the mountain tops. This, too, was a sign that the fire of the underworld awaited those men who did not fear the gods.

When they are put together in the sequence given above, the biblical narratives are seen to be fairly straightforward descriptions of what actually happened. Virtually the only interpretive parts of the various stories are those parts which try to show *why* God decided to destroy the earth. In the same way, the creation myths of the other continents lose a great deal of their mythological character and may be considered as truthful reporting of events as they were seen in different parts of the world.

As it stands, the story is simply factual. However spine-chilling the events described may be, they do not constitute a symbol when they are viewed as a sequence. It is only later, when the process can be looked at dispassionately as a unity that its symbolic character arises.

The unitive concept of creation which is formed in the minds of later generations of men when they digest the reports of their ancestors is of a *pattern*. Three heavenly bodies or gods stir up the elements, of which there are four; *earth*, which shakes and rumbles and splits apart; *fire*, which rains down from heaven, pours out from the earth, and consumes everything in its path; *air*, which tears up the trees, fans the flames of the fire and drives the water of the flood before it; and *water*, which pours down from the skies, covers the earth and even quenches the fire. In the chaotic description, there is nothing except these four elements in torment. Even the heavenly bodies can no longer be seen, but that they are the cause of the maelstrom of the elements is never doubted.

Three gods and four elements; what does this *mean*?

The moment the question is asked, the number exists as a full-blown symbol, for every symbol incorporates a mystery and, as man finds an answer to one question raised by his symbols, more mysteries and more questions arise and abstraction proceeds apace.

What makes man ask the first question which creates the symbol? He asks it because he sees in the symbol something which reminds him of sub-consciously-realised Truth. This is what makes a symbol what it is; there is a correspondence of pattern between the concrete symbol and the abstract Truth it represents. So the first response of man is to search for correspondences between the symbol and other parts of the phenomenal world. This is rationalisation by *discovery*.

Here, says the seeker, are seven things which are inseparable from creation. What else groups itself in a similar way? Look, there are seven planets! Is this coincidence? No, in an ordered world there is no such thing as pure coincidence, so the fact must be significant. A line taken from the centre point of a circle to its circumference divides the circle into six exactly-equal parts when used as a chord, making seven points in all; there is a correspondence between these points and the 'planets'. Miraculous! Seven is three plus four; three *times* four is twelve; if I divide a rope into twelve equal portions by means of knots and then stretch it out to form a triangle so that the sides are three, four and five units long, the angle between the sides which are three and four units long is exactly a right angle; but three plus four is my original seven. Another miracle! It is a miracle which enables me to build a pyramid whose sides are accurately aligned to within a fraction of a degree of a right angle.

From the initial discovery of such correspondences, whole sciences are developed. Astronomy became a science when it was discovered how to divide the heavens into equal parts; building became an accurate science as soon as man learned how to construct a right angle.

But the search for correspondences is not only a matter of discovery. Man imposes the ideal pattern on nature creatively as well. He decides that there are seven wonders of the world, seven oceans, seven sins, seven virtues and seven metals corresponding with the planets forming a 'transmutation ladder' from lead to gold. This is rationalisation by *invention* and, from this process, another set of sciences has grown. Alchemy becomes chemistry; 'planetary atomics' becomes physics, electronics, nucleonics; number magic becomes the calculus, statistics, relativity theory. A mighty superstructure based on superstition? No, this is the Truth showing glimpses of its many faces in unexpected ways because one of its symbols was pursued when its character was subconsciously recognised. For serendipity is the rule rather than the exception in science. Almost every major discovery has been made by scientists *who were looking for something else*, or who arrived at correct conclusions as a result of faulty reasoning, in pursuit of what was, for them, a symbol of Truth. Such is the power of a true symbol that it gradually yields up its secrets in spite of the ineptness of the seeker.

While the magicians, priests and scientists are busy with their discoveries and inventions, the philosopher takes up the symbol and tries to see its Truth in a more direct fashion. The correspondences he looks for are abstract. So he takes apart in his mind the triad of gods which was once a trio of celestial bodies and reconstructs them as *principles*. Thus, they become the principles of masculinity, femininity and love or attraction, or, in other minds, they become the *gunas* of the Hindus; or he may see them in terms of the primary colours which, when mixed, make all the rest, or the primary consonances of music, the octave, the fifth and the fourth, which create all the other notes, and he tries to 'see' the creative principles involved.

At the same time, he analyses the four 'elements' not as *things* (which is the job of the scientist), but as pure *forms* and, by analogy with the four cardinal points of the compass, he decides that they represent polarisation in two dimensions. But polarisation is inherent in the principles of masculinity and femininity. It is therefore polarisation which drives the elements apart and the third principle, attraction, which holds them together and maintains them in being.

Thus, says the philosopher, is the world of multiplicity formed out of Unity. Creation is threefold in principle and fourfold in appearance. So the septenary displays another facet of its Truth to an enquiring mind.

Yet the symbol itself retains its mystery. Whenever it answers a question, it asks another, and this is its force.

Appendix 1

The Constant Elements of the Creation Myths

Most creation myths which are part of the cultural background of particular tribes are concerned to show how the tribe originated and so the main characters in each story are likely to be the tribal gods or culture heros. To some extent, this also applies to the recorded myths of whole nations, particularly those nations which, because of their geographical isolation, have historically had little contact with the rest of humanity.

It is necessary, therefore, to tread warily when trying to relate these gods or heroes to cosmic events. Nevertheless, the correspondences which occur between the myths of widely separated cultures, and more especially when cataclysmic events are mentioned, are close enough to suggest common origins. In many cases, this community of origin may simply be due to common ancestors or direct communication in the past between peoples who are now isolated from each other. In other cases, such an explanation is unlikely and we must then adopt the view that the correspondences are due to a sharing of similar experiences by people in different parts of the world.

In any case, the method of analysis of the constantly-occurring elements of the various creation myths which we have adopted here is to assume that the stories represent the remnants of original eye-witness reports. Any other assumption is illogical. Men do make up stories for the amusement of their fellows, but these usually have a comparatively short life. They are not told with the same conviction as those in which *facts* are related and the listener is not often in any doubt that the stories are fiction. He is unlikely, therefore, to repeat them and they tend to die a natural death after a few tellings.

The one element which is common to almost all creation myths is the Deluge. Few people would now deny that we are here dealing with factual events. The only question which remains open is whether a single, world-wide inundation is being described or whether different areas of the world were flooded at different times. Geological evidence, as now understood, suggests the latter, largely on the grounds of the type of cultural artifacts found above and below the deposits believed to have been left by floods in various parts of the world. There is, however, no single time-scale by which these layers may be judged, especially when we are dealing with a period of a few thousand years. It is even possible that the innundation related in the myths was of a quite different character from those which left deep deposits, being more in the nature of a tidal wave sweeping over the land and draining off again in a comparatively short time so that its deposits would be scarcely recognisable to a geologist.

The internal evidence of the myths themselves suggests strongly that a single event, or a series of connected events, affecting the whole world in a greater or lesser degree, is involved.

Source Material

The material for analysis is almost entirely immediately-recognisable as descriptions of catastrophic events. In classical mythology, there are many stories which may be *interpreted* relating to such events, but we shall not, in the main, use such material except when it clearly shows unmistakeable correspondences of both form and detail with the more direct narratives.

Europe and the Middle East are represented by Sumerian, Egyptian, Nordic, Celtic, Phoenician, Lithuanian, Persian and Biblical sources; the Americas by the myths of the indigenous peoples, mainly Red Indian; India by Vedantic sources; the Far East by Chinese and Japanese myths; the Southern Seas by Polynesian and Melanesian myths. Africa south of the Sahara is not represented because the African peoples in general do not seem to have any recognisable creation stories. Whether this is due to the characteristics of the African races themselves or whether it means that the greater part of Africa missed the more severe effects of the world-catastrophe, is an open question.

North and South America

The Indian races indigenous to both North and South America are often thought of as a single ethnic group, but their types and languages vary as much as those of the races of Africa. Culturally, they are ultra-conservative and we may be sure that many of their tribal myths have been handed down orally from father to son with very little variation for innumerable generations. In some areas, there has been a considerable admixture of African blood which has helped to determine the ethnic type but, except for those mixtures whose African element is comparatively recent, this is not reflected in the mythology of the people. Accordingly, we shall treat the Americas as a single mythological group.

(1) WASHO INDIAN CREATION MYTH (CALIFORNIA)
A great earthquake sets the mountains on fire. The flames reach to the sky and melt the stars, which fall on the earth. A flood follows, from which men try to escape by building a high tower, but the men are changed into stones.

(2) and (3) TUPI-GUARANI MYTHS (BRAZIL)
(a) Monan decides to destroy the world by fire, but his fires are extinguished by great rains caused by Irin Mage.
(b) A different myth from the same region says that Toroguenket, the moon, periodically falls on the earth and destroys it except for the parts which are saved by the intervention of Toroshompek, the sun.

(4) IROQUOIS INDIAN MYTH
Athensic, the mother of all men, fell from the sky during the time the flood was receding. The land on which she found herself became a great continent. When their life had become organised, the Iroquois left this abode for the land of the stone giants. They met various enemies on the way, but these were conquered by the thunder god and his brother, the west wind.

(5) BOLIVIAN MYTH
During a great conflagration, some men took shelter in a cave. The fire was followed by a flood, which destroyed all that had been spared from the burning. The flood blocked the entrance to the cave and the survivors had tremendous difficulty in getting out.

These examples are representative of a great number of the creation-myths of the Americas, in which the names of the gods are

CONSTANT ELEMENTS OF CREATION MYTHS

different, while the cataclysmic details vary only in the number of them which are mentioned. Of some 34 myths examined, 30 mentioned a flood, 13 a fire, 7 caves, 3 falling rocks or falling stars and four of the myths mentioned a falling moon or implied that the moon was the cause of the catastrophe. Other elements mentioned in one or more legends and which, as we shall see, occur in myths from other continents are: towers, great stones, stone men, men made from clay, earthquakes and great winds.

The Far East
(6) THE KOJI-KI JAPANESE LEGEND
In the beginning, In and Yo (cf. Chinese Yin and Yang) were in the cosmic egg. The egg split into two pieces, which became heaven and earth. The earth floated on the waters. Seven generations of gods were born before the first human pair who, looking down from the bridge of heaven, stirred up the waters with a *jewelled spear*, whereupon the island of Onogoro arose and the flood receded. The pair settled on the island and had four children, who were the sun goddess, the moon god, the sea god and the fire god.

(7) THE CHINESE LEGEND OF KUNG-KUNG
Matter from the primeval chaos polarised itself into Yang and Yin, from which came Pan-Ku, the giant, whose body produced the earth, the planets and the stars. Kung-Kung, the dragon, butted down the pillars of heaven with his head, which caused the collapse of the firmament and the release of the waters above it. From this, the world was flooded.

The South Pacific
(8) GILBERT ISLAND MYTH
In the dim past, a terrible darkness came over the earth and, in the darkness, the god of floods made the waters rise and cover the land.

(9) CELEBES ISLAND MYTH
The earth was covered by a great flood, which destroyed everything except the rice, which enabled the tribe to survive when the waters subsided.

(10) THE TAHITI MYTH
There was a flood in which only one man and one woman survived by climbing the highest mountain on the island. They had a son and daughter who were the ancestors of all Tahitians.

Northern Europe
(11) NORDIC CREATION MYTH
The world began as chaos between the northern ice and the southern fire. The three sons of Bor killed the giant Ymir and the giant's body became the world, while his blood became a great flood.

(12) PROSE EDDA LEGEND
The story of the Ragnarok relates how, for seven successive winters, the sun gives no warmth. A great battle between the celestial gods occurs. The sun is hidden by a wolf, the earth shakes and the sea rushes over it. The last of the 'frost giants' escape in a ship. Meanwhile the 'planetary gods' are killing each other. The moon hell-gog and Tyr fight to the death of both. Surt, one of the giants, shoots flames over the earth, most of which is destroyed. After the battle subsides, men reappear on the earth, the sun has a daughter and darkness is banished for ever.

(13) IRISH CELTIC CREATION MYTH
Six of the legendary heroes escape the world-flood to Innisfail in a ship. They are killed, however, when a large red moon appears, with bright, expanding clouds, and breaks up into a hundred pieces.

India and Asia
(14) MYTH FROM RIG VEDA 1, 32A, v. 3, 7 and 8

> Like a vehement bull, he (Indra) took to himself the Soma,
> Drank the pressed drink from three mighty bowls,
> Picked up his weapon, the fiery bolt,
> And slew the first-born dragon.
>
> Footless, handless, he gave battle to Indra,
> Who flung the bolt on his back.
> And the gelded bull who had saught to equal the virile bull,
> Vritra, lay scattered in many places.

And over him who lay there like a slaughtered offering,
The flood of the waters climbed,
Which he, by his might, had formerly enclosed.
Beneath its course, now, the great dragon lay.

(15) MYTH FROM THE MAHABHARATA
In those days, the powerful chariot-riding King of Gods, surrounded by his army of celestials, saw before him the great titan, standing mighty as a mountain, 4500 miles tall and in girth a full 1500. Whereupon ... the entire host was paralysed with fear, and their leader, discerning the contour of his foe, lost the use of his limbs from the waist down. ...

The war commenced. And it terrified all three worlds. For the whole sky was covered with the warriors of both sides, wielding swords, javelins, ... rocks of various sizes, ... numerous kinds of celestial weapons, fires and burning brands. ...

Then ... Vritra deftly overwhelmed both the King of Gods and the entire world of air with a dense shower of rocks. And the gods, burning with anger, pouring a shower of arrows at those rocks, dissolved them. ... The King of Gods then said, '... I shall now, with this my thunderbolt, slay the invincible son of the mother of demons. ...'

And the gods ..., seeing the enemy struck with that fever, lifted a roar of great joy. ... And the form that the King of Gods then assumed, ... was such that none could look on it without great fear.

But let us first tell of the stricken titan. When he had been filled with that burning fever, his immense mouth gave forth a blast of flame. His colour disappeared. Everywhere he trembled ... and each hair on his body stood erect. His mind came through his jaws in the shape of an evil, hideous jackal, and meteors burst blazing from his sides. ...

And the King of Gods watched the monster, who ... yawned wide with a great howl; and, while his mouth was still open, the god let fly into it his bolt filled with no less energy than the fire that consumes the universe at the end of a cosmic cycle — which blasted Vritra forthwith ... And the King of Gods ... made away in haste in his chariot toward the sky.

(16) LITHUANIAN MYTH
Floods covered the earth, but Pramzimas dropped a nutshell from the sky, which became a ship. The ship enabled one man and one woman to survive.

North Africa and the Near East

(17) ANCIENT EGYPTIAN MYTH

Ra ordered Hathor (a lunar goddess) and Sekhmet (fire goddess) to destroy the people of the earth, who had offended him. Later, he relented but, being unable to stop them carrying out his earlier order, he decided to make them drunk and so forget about their task. With this purpose, he flooded the world with beer.

(18) THE PHOENICIAN LEGEND OF SANCHUNIATHON

Wind and Desire, the progenitors of the Cosmic Egg, Mot, arose from the pre-existing Air and Chaos. The egg opened and released the sun, the moon and the stars. Light separated the waters from the sky.

(19) THE SUMERIAN EPIC OF PARADISE, THE FLOOD AND THE FALL OF MAN

This story is close in detail to the biblical version which, however, has been purged of some of the creator gods of the Sumerian myth. It tells how the world was produced by the goddess of the primeval ocean. Man was made from clay by an earth-mother and a sea goddess, with the advice of a water-god of wisdom. The following is a translation by Stephen Langdon of the section describing the flood:

'From the foundations of heaven a black cloud arose. Adad roared in it. The tumult of Adad ascends to the skies. All that is bright is turned to darkness, and brother sees brother no more. The folk of the skies can no longer recognise each other. The gods feared the flood. They fled, they climbed into the heaven of Anu. The gods crouched like a dog on a wall, they lay down.

'For six nights and days wind and flood marched on, the hurricane subdued the land. When the seventh day dawned, the hurricane was abated, the flood which had waged war like an army. The sea was stilled, its voice was silent and all mankind was turned into mud.'

Biblical Myths

(20) THE DESTRUCTION OF SODOM AND GOMORRAH

The two angels came to Sodom in the evening, and Lot was sitting in the gateway of the city.... He said 'I pray you, sirs, turn aside to my humble home ... you can rise early and continue your journey....' Before they lay down to sleep, the men of Sodom, both young and old, surrounded the house — everyone without exception. ... 'Bring them out,' they shouted, 'so that we may have intercourse with them.'

Lot went to the doorway to them ... and said 'No, my friends ... do not touch these men, because they have come under the shelter of my roof.' They said 'Out of our way! This man has come and settled here as an alien, and does he now take it upon himself to judge us? We will treat you worse than them.' They crowded in on the man Lot and pressed close to smash in the door. But the two men inside reached out, pulled Lot in, and closed the door. Then they struck the men in the doorway with blindness, both small and great, so that they could not find the door.

The two men said to Lot 'Have you anyone else here ... who belongs to you in the city? Get them out of this place, because we are going to destroy it. . . .'

As soon as it was dawn, the angels urged Lot to go ... and they took him by the hand ... and ... led him on until he was outside of the city. When they had brought them out, they said 'Flee ... to the hills or you will be swept away. . . .'

The sun had risen over the land as Lot entered Zoar; and then the Lord rained down fire and brimstone from the skies on Sodom and Gomorrah. He overthrew those cities and destroyed all the plain, with everyone living there and everything growing in the ground. But Lot's wife, behind him, looked back, and she turned into a pillar of salt. . . .

Lot went up from Zoar and settled in the hill-country with his two daughters ... in a cave. The elder daughter said to the younger, 'Our father is old and there is not a man in the country to come to us in the usual way. Come now, let us make our father drink wine and then lie with him and, in this way, keep the family alive through our father.'

(21) THE TOWER OF BABEL

Once upon a time all the world spoke a single language and used the same words. As men journeyed in the east, they came upon a plain in the land of Sinar and settled there. . . . 'Come,' they said, 'let us build ourselves a city and a tower with its top in the heavens, and make a name for ourselves, or we shall be dispersed all over the earth.' Then the Lord came down to see the city and tower which mortal men had built, and he said, 'Here they are, one people with a single language, and now they have started to do this; henceforward nothing they have a mind to do will be beyond their reach. Come, let us go down there and confuse their speech, so that they will not understand what they say to one another.' So the Lord dispersed them from there all over the earth.

(22) THE FLOOD

Towards the end of seven days the waters of the flood came on the earth ... all the springs of the great abyss broke through, the windows of the sky were opened, and rain fell on the earth for forty days and forty nights, and the waters swelled and lifted up the ark so that it rose high above the ground. They swelled and increased over the earth ... until they covered all the high mountains everywhere under heaven ... to a depth of fifteen cubits. Every living creature that moves on the earth perished....

When the waters had increased for a hundred and fifty days, God ... made a wind pass over the earth, and the waters began to subside.

(23) GENESIS

In the beginning of creation, when God made heaven and earth, the earth was without form and void, with darkness over the face of the abyss, and a mighty wind that swept over the surface of the waters. God said 'Let there be light ...' and he separated light from darkness ... the first day.

God said, 'Let there be a vault between the waters ...' and separated the water under the vault from the water above it ... a second day.

God said, 'Let the waters under the heaven be gathered into one place, so that dry land may appear.... Let the earth produce fresh growth.' ... a third day.

God ... made the two great lights, the greater to govern the day and the lesser to govern the night; and with them he made the stars ... a fourth day.

God ... created the great sea-monsters and all living creatures that move and swarm in the waters, ... a fifth day.

God .. made wild animals, cattle and reptiles ... created man in his own image ... a sixth day.

Thus heaven and earth were completed with all their mighty throng ... and on the seventh day he ceased from all his work.

The Catastrophic Elements

If we assume a single series of events as the basis of all the catastrophic elements related in the myths, it is natural that floods should be described more often than any other feature, for a big enough movement of water would affect all countries whereas fires, earthquakes and bodies falling from the sky, being events isolated to a place

CONSTANT ELEMENTS OF CREATION MYTHS

and time in each case, will be reported less often. Extending this argument, we must not, then, assume that, because a particular element is mentioned only once or twice, it is unrelated to the other, more common features. The task before us is to find a single cause, or a series of related causes, for all the elements which appear.

(a) THE FLOOD
In myths 1, 2(a), 4, 5, 11, 14 and 17, the flood follows a fire. The order of the stories in the Bible reverses this sequence but, since the fire and flood stories are quite distinct and separate, the order in which they appear in the writings as now collected does not necessarily reflect the temporal order of the events themselves.

Those creation myths which begin with water are usually concerned with the re-emergence of life *after* the catastrophe and less so with the nature of the prior events. This applies particularly to the Genesis story of creation (23), where the first image is of an abyss of water over which the wind blows.

The flood is not necessarily the last destructive event. In 3, the moon falls to earth as the flood is receding; in 13, the moon explodes during or after the flood; in 16, the nutshell drops from the sky during the flood.

The deluge is usually attributed to the wrath of a god as it is in the story of Noah. This is an obvious form in which the event could be expected to be rationalised. In 4, the causal agent is the moon goddess; in 7, the dragon butts down the pillars of heaven, while in 14, the dragon causes the flood by being killed, his force having previously held the waters back; in 17, the lunar goddess is the direct cause of the fire but only indirectly the cause of the flood.

The fact that, when a physical cause is suggested in the myths, this is usually lunar, is not in itself surprising because the ancients were obviously aware of the connection between the moon and the tides. But why should the moon be also the cause of fire? Note also that, if we are to consider the dragon as lunar, we are dealing with a moon which breathes fire. This is surely not the moon with which we are familiar but a *different* lunar body, one which fell to earth during the events described.

(b) THE CONFLAGRATION
In 1, the fire is caused by an earthquake; in 12, the fire follows the flood and is the result of a celestial battle; in 14, with the more

common fire-flood sequence, a fiery bolt from above is the cause; in 15, the celestial dragon falls to earth in flames.

In the myths which do not specifically mention fire, the conditions just before the flood are usually described as intense darkness with very black clouds. Now, while dark clouds are the natural accompaniment of very heavy rains, they are referred to with such emphasis as to suggest that they are not ordinary rain clouds. Possibly, they are the smoke and steam clouds caused by the fires burning around the globe.

(c) EARTHQUAKES

Earthquakes and volcanic activity of tremendous proportions are described or implied in several myths, notably in 1, 7 and 12.

(d) CELESTIAL ACTIVITY

Two main types of activity are involved: first, there are the descriptions of what can be seen going on in the sky as a prelude or accompaniment to the events on earth; secondly, the *direct* effects on earth, i.e. things which fall from the sky. Some of the visual descriptions are very vivid:

> The stars melt in the flames and fall to earth (1)
> The moon falls on the earth and destroys it (2)
> Something falls from the sky and becomes a continent (3)
> Light comes from the sky *in pieces* (4)
> The moon goddess causes the flood and is then put up in the sky as our present moon, the earth having 'been without a moon' (4)
> The cosmic egg (moon?) splits into two pieces (6) (18)
> The firmament collapses (7)
> A celestial giant is killed, his body becoming earth, his blood a great flood (11)
> The sun is 'hidden by a wolf' (12)
> The moon hell-dog fights with another celestial body, both being destroyed. A celestial body shoots flames on the earth (12)
> A moon explodes, killing those on earth (13)
> Two celestial bodies, represented as solar and lunar, fight in 14 and 15. In one, the body which is eventually destroyed is first described as 'footless, handless and gelded', in the other, it has a 'yawning mouth', suggesting a piece torn out of it. Later, it lies scattered in pieces on the earth. Other effects described are: fire shooting from the body's mouth, then something of hideous

shape emerging from it, meteors bursting from its sides and, finally, its blasting by a bolt.

A lunar object with fire burns up the earth in 17.

In 20, two angels (celestial bodies) are involved in the rain of fire and brimstone from the heavens. This image is echoed in the cherubim with fiery swords invoked when Adam is banished from Eden.

A nutshell drops from the sky in 16 and becomes a ship. The ship image is of *half* a nutshell, which corresponds to the visual image of the yawning mouth of the dragon.

(e) CAVES

Caves are mentioned usually in the fire myths, as in the story of Lot. In the few cases where they are mentioned in connection with floods, the fire or falling rocks can be inferred since a cave is no protection against a flood.

(f) TOWERS, PILLARS AND STONE MEN

The building of a high tower to escape the flood is mentioned in 1. This is strange because the same story starts with earthquakes, which would be disastrous to a tower. The builders are turned to stone.

The stated object of the tower-building in 21 is to prevent the people being 'dispersed over the earth'.

Lot's wife is turned into a *pillar* of salt (20).

Many flood stories speak of men being turned into mud or clay, while others describe men as being *created* from mud after the flood subsides. In 3, the people migrate to the land of the stone giants.

While it may not be important to the main catastrophe theme, we are impelled to find a reason for these odd images which intrude into an otherwise clear picture. There is an obvious similarity of image between towers, pillars and stone men, the main difference being one of the relative size. We are reminded of the great carved images of Easter Island, huge elongated rocks standing on end, with the lower part buried in the earth, the features having probably been carved *in situ* by men who saw resemblances to human features in the natural stones. The only explanation which fits the rest of the picture is that all the towers, pillars and stone men are the rocks fallen from the sky mentioned in several of the myths, discovered by men after the catastrophe and explained by them in various ways.

Synthesis of the Cosmic Event

What can cause floods on an intercontinental scale? Not simply rain, because the normal causes of rain are self-limiting in their effects. Rain of exceptional spread and duration could be caused by widespread fires, the heat of which might continuously recycle the water vapour. But rain can only cause serious flooding when it falls over an extensive 'catchment area' and then runs down into a 'basin'. It could not cause the submersion of islands.

While rain might cause limited flooding, therefore, we must look for a great movement of the sea to account for floods of the scale called for. The melting of the polar ice has sometimes been invoked as a possible cause for the raising of the general level of the seas, but this would be a gradual process, if it ever occurred. It would not appear as a catastrophe. Only a tremendous explosion under the ocean or the impact of a large body from space striking the earth in the middle of one of the oceans could generate tidal waves large enough to cause world-wide catastrophic flooding. Since this cause is explicitly mentioned by the myths themselves in several cases, we have to adopt it as the main cause of the floods. Can the arrival of such a body from space account for all the phenomena described in the myths? Let us consider the event in phases and note the probable effect on earth of each phase.

1. *An asteroid, or similar celestial body, with a very eccentric orbit round the sun enters the immediate vicinity of the earth in such a way that, for a period, the two bodies are in almost parallel orbits. The gravitation of the earth is now enough to change the path of the asteroid so that it begins to orbit the earth itself in a contracting spiral.* The first effect of the approach of this body on earth would be a change in the tides as the gravity due to it alternately reduced and reinforced the tidal effects of the sun and moon.

Visually, the body would appear at first like a dim star, then, by the time it was the same distance from the earth as the moon, it would look like a very bright planet and when it had reached an orbit much smaller than that of the moon, it would have the appearance of a second moon. It would appear to move much more rapidly through the sky than the moon, going through its phases in a day or so. Later, of course, it would look much larger than the moon and might eclipse the sun ('hidden by the wolf') at odd times. By this time, its tidal effects on the sea would be enormous, with disastrous flooding of low-lying areas of the land.

CONSTANT ELEMENTS OF CREATION MYTHS 167

2. *The spiral orbit eventually brings the body into the rarified outer layers of the earth's atmosphere. The friction heats its outer surface to red heat.*

The 'second moon' is now huge in the sky. When it is lit by the sun, it is pale in colour, but when it is in its dark phase or when it is eclipsed by the earth (quite often now that it is so close) it appears a threatening red. This is why it is said to 'lose its colour' in going through its phases.

Great tides now sweep over many land areas, but are not high enough to reach the hills. This is why some accounts have floods preceding the fires from heaven.

3. *The body reaches a critical level in its orbit at which the combined effects of gravitational stress and heat shear off one whole section of it. The smaller part separates from its parent, leaving a gaping hole and, being now thrust into an even lower orbit, becomes white-hot and shatters into thousands of pieces of all sizes.*

To an observer on earth, this would have been a sight to strike terror into him and would certainly give the impression of a celestial battle.

4. *The debris of the exploded part descends to earth, the smaller grains burning up as meteors, while the larger rocks reach the surface, some falling on land and some into the sea.*

The result of the explosion of the body is to make the individual rocks travel in all directions outward from the centre of the explosion, so that they will all descend with different speeds and on different parts of the surface of the earth. Thus the effects observed will have considerable variation.

The dust and small grains will be seen as showers of shooting stars, many of which will explode in the sky in trails of fire. Some of the really large rocks with high impact speeds will create huge craters like the well-known circular crater in Arizona. Some, falling into the sea, will add to the havoc already being wrought by the tides. Still others, descending with less force through flood waters, may lie on the surface or be only partially buried in the mud.

Many of these partially-buried rocks will be exposed to view when the waters subside. Their shapes will often be elongated since, in the initial explosion, they will have sheared along parallel lines of weakness in the parent body. Their shapes will have been modified due to the burning friction of the air during their descent.

Other effects which will be noted by those observers who live to tell their stories will include:

(a) As white-hot stones descend in the forests, fires will break out which will spread unchecked over huge areas.
(b) Clouds of black smoke will hide the heavens. Where fire and water meet, the smoke and steam will rise together over the intense heat, forming great thunder clouds, leading to fierce cloudbursts in a repeating cycle. Thunder, lightning and torrential rains, with hurricane-strength winds, will lash the earth continuously.
(c) Every impact of a meteorite will be felt as an earthquake and, where the crust of the earth is weakened, volcanic eruptions will break out.

5. *The final cosmic event is the descent of the remaining section of the asteroid, which strikes the earth in the middle of one of the oceans.*
It is, of course, much more likely that impact would take place in the sea than on land because the sea area is so much greater. Even so, the first effect would be to make the whole earth shudder. The ocean will be blasted away from the centre of the impact with a force of ten thousand hydrogen bombs. A circular wall of water a mile high will spread out from the blast point, submerging everything in its path. Whole sections of continents will disappear below the raging waters. Reaction waves will be set up in all the oceans and flood will follow flood.

The already-weakened crust of the earth is further split and the volcano and earthquake belts we know today are formed.

At last, the effects begin to die down and the water drains from the land, leaving a world covered in mud. Life emerges slowly and picks up where it left off in a scarcely-recognisable world.

Given the one unexpected event, all the other effects follow. A careful reading of the quoted myths will show that every circumstance described or inferred is accounted for.

Just how unlikely is it that the initial event could occur?

In 1937, the asteroid Hermes passed within 400,000 miles of the earth, a distance comparable with that of the moon. Several of the known asteroids have orbits which carry them well within the orbit of the earth and at least one actually approaches closer to the sun than Mercury! Naturally, even when an asteroid has an orbit which at one

CONSTANT ELEMENTS OF CREATION MYTHS 169

point closely parallels that of the earth, the chances of both bodies reaching this particular point on their orbits at the same moment are very slight, *but this almost happened in the case of Hermes in 1937!* Some 4000 asteroids are known and there must be thousands not yet discovered. Over a period of several thousand years, it would be surprising if near coincidences had not happened many times. The capture of one of these bodies is therefore not impossible or even improbable.

The records of the peoples of the earth in the form of creation myths show clearly that it *did* happen. No other circumstance can account for all phenomena described and by no stretch of imagination can we conceive that each of these stories was separately invented by man for his own amusement.

Appendix 2

The Antediluvian Patriarch List

By what criteria are we to decide the significance or otherwise of the numbers in the Genesis patriarchal list quoted on page 69 in a sense other than a purely historical one?

Genealogies abound in the Bible and seem to have been important even for the humblest of the Jews, who used them to identify themselves with a particular tribe. Why, then, should we not accept the patriarch-list at its face value, whether considered mythical or not?

The first reason for rejecting this explanation is the nature of the numbers used as the supposed ages of the patriarchs. In other parts of the Bible, where ages are mentioned, they are reasonable ones within the normally accepted life-span of three-score and ten years.

It may be thought natural enough to exaggerate the ages of a line of patriarchs on the grounds that this adds to their stature but, if this were the intention, why should Adam be shown as relinquishing the leadership to a series of successors during his own supposed lifetime?

There are also inconsistencies in the manner in which the ages are allocated. No fewer than 13 of the 30 ages mentioned are divisible by 10. This would be a reasonable way of rounding off the figures if it were applied throughout, but we find mixed with the multiples of 10 a number of *too exact* figures, like 969, 807 etc.

I have mentioned that there is always a common factor in the age of the patriarch when his successor is born and the years he lives afterwards; reasonable enough if rounding off were the intention, but then *the same* common factor would appear throughout.

The ages are given in the list below with their common factors, showing how these vary from patriarch to patriarch.

There is thus no escaping the conclusion that the numbers relate to something other than their stated meaning. But to what do they allude?

The reader may already have noticed that the form in which the figures are given bears a striking resemblance to those in the Cuneiform tablet (Plimpton 322, mentioned on page 76) which, as we saw, are the integral units measuring the sides of right-angled triangles.

THE ANTEDILUVIAN PATRIARCH LIST

NO.	YEARS BEFORE SUCCESSOR	YEARS AFTER SUCCESSOR	AGE AT DEATH
1	10 x 13	10 x 80	10 x 93
2	3 x 35	3 x 269	3 x 304
3	5 x 18	5 x 163	5 x 181
4	70 x 1	70 x 12	70 x 13
5	5 x 13	5 x 166	5 x 179
6	2 x 81	2 x 400	2 x 481
7	5 x 13	5 x 60	5 x 73
8	17 x 11	17 x 46	17 x 57
9	7 x 26	7 x 85	7 x 111
10	50 x 12	50 x 7	50 x 19

Each of the patriarchal ages is listed in the form a + b = c. It would, if we were to consider this as the source of the list, be necessary to take the square root of each number as the length of a side of a triangle. Rather disappointingly, no perfect squares occur among the ages.

However, if we reduce the ages of the sixth patriarch by their common factor, they become 81, 400, 481, where both 81 and 400 are perfect squares (of 9 and 20 respectively). Their sum is not, however, a perfect square.

On the basis of this rather nebulous evidence, we nevertheless extract the square roots of each patriarch's ages reduced by their common factor, construct the 10 triangles and determine the angle included between the hypotenuse and the adjacent sides, with the following result:

	a^2	b^2	c^2	a	b	c	Included Angle
1.	13	80	93	3.606	8.944	9.644	21° 58'
2.	35	269	304	5.916	16.401	17.436	19° 50'
3.	18	163	181	4.243	12.767	13.454	18° 23'
4.	1	12	13	1.000	3.464	3.606	16° 6'
5.	13	166	179	3.606	12.844	13.380	15° 38'
6.	81	400	481	9.000	20.000	21.932	24° 14'
7.	13	60	73	3.606	7.746	8.544	24° 58'
8.	11	46	57	3.317	6.782	7.550	26° 4'
9.	26	85	111	5.099	9.220	10.536	28° 57'
10.	12	7	19	3.464	2.646	4.359	52° 38'

At once, we see a pattern which was not obvious from an examination of the original figures. Starting at the top of the list, the angle diminishes in fairly steady steps until we reach patriarch number 5. Here it jumps to an angle greater than the first and starts increasing by similar steps up to number 9, where it again jumps to an angle almost double the previous one (and, as a matter of interest, very close to the pyramid angle of about one seventh of a complete revolution).

If this series of angles is intentional, what purpose would warrant its being recorded in the book of Genesis?

Here, we shall have to move into the realm of pure conjecture. We know that the list concerns events leading up to the Flood. Suppose we consider it as a set of astronomical observations by means of which the ancient priests attempted to predict the time of the coming catastrophe. Perhaps in this way, we can make sense of both the figures themselves and their literary context.

Angles which change in a fairly regular way in astronomical observation normally refer to the sun, moon and planets, whose positions change in the sky, while those of the stars do not. The body most likely to be connected with floods is, of course, the moon, so we assume as our starting point that each angle represents a lunar observation, say, the azimuth angle between due east and the position of the moon at its rising. This would account for the comparatively small total variation in the angles all except for the last one. Now this last angle, so noticeably different from the rest, is Noah's *and therefore coincides with the advent of the Flood*. This sudden change of angle is the justification for the whole set of figures. It is as if the astronomers were putting on record that the advent of the Flood was heralded by the moonrise taking place $20°$ away from its expected position!

But what moon are we talking about? Let us read the wording of the list again. It says, in effect, 'This figure represents the time at which patriarch A begat patriarch B'. If this refers to a moon whose angle we are measuring, we can only read into the wording the statement that *the first moon is followed by a second moon* and that the angle between their risings is such and such an angle.

Since their orbits and periods are different, we shall expect their relative positions at rising to vary steadily from observation to observation. At some stage, however, they will be $180°$ out of phase and then, from an observational point of view they will appear to change places, with a consequent change in the sense of the angle between them, hence the break in the middle of the table.

THE ANTEDILUVIAN PATRIARCH LIST

The reason for there being 10 angles to measure depends on the relative periods of the two 'moons'. We must suppose that these were related in such a way that in 10 days the period of the one 'caught up' with that of the other so that their relative cycles were repeated, making 10 consecutive observations of the double rising sufficient to ensure that there had been no significant change in their relationship since the previous cycle. Possibly, we should think of *nine* observations as being related to the regular cycle, while Noah's being so radically different, recalls a single observation which convinced the priests that catastrophe was upon them.

How do we account for the difference in the wording of Enoch's disappearance? Remember, Enoch does not die but 'was seen no more, because God had taken him away'. In astronomical terms, this strongly suggests an eclipse preventing some part of the observation taking place at this stage. If this interpretation is correct, we are dealing not with regularly-recurring cycles but with a single unique set of observations recorded by the astronomers prior to the catastrophe and preserved for posterity in the belief that it might aid some future observer should he be faced with a similar set of circumstances.

The facts are these:
1. We know the original king lists on which the biblical list is based to have been compiled by the ancient Babylonian or Sumerian priests.
2. We know they were skilled in astronomical observation.
3. We know they compiled lists of figures representing Pythagorean triangles for the purpose of describing angles.
4. We know that the king and patriarch lists lead up to the Flood and, in the latter case, produce a set of angles displaying a regular progression.

Any extrapolation from these facts is bound to be conjecture, but it would I think be hard to find a more plausible explanation than the one I have suggested.

Bibliography

The Masks of God: Oriental Mythology, by J. Campbell (Secker and Warburg, 1962).
The Wisdom Tree, by E. Hawkridge (Houghton Mifflin Co., 1965).
Everyman's Dictionary of Non-Classical Mythology, compiled by E. Sykes (J. M. Dent and Sons, 1965).
The Encyclopaedia of Myths and Legends of All Nations, by H. S. Robinson and K. Wilson (Kaye and Ward Ltd., 1962).
A Dictionary of Symbols, by J. E. Cirlot; trans. J. Sage (Philosophical Library Inc., 1962).
Myths, Dreams and Mysteries, by M. Eliade; trans. P. Mairet (Fontana Library of Theology and Philosophy, 1968).
The Golden Bough, by J. G. Frazer, abridged edition (Macmillan and Co., 1949).
The Treasury of Mathematics, Vol. 1, by H. Midonick (Penguin Books, 1968).
The Pyramids of Egypt, by I. E. S. Edwards (Penguin Books, 1947).
The Archaeology of Palestine, by W. F. Albright (Penguin Books, 1947).
Voices in Stone, by E. Doblhofer (Souvenir Press, 1961).
Alchemical Studies, the Collected Works of C. G. Jung; trans. R. F. C. Hull (Routledge and Kegan Paul, 1967).
Memories, Dreams and Reflections, by C. G. Jung with A. Jaffé; trans. R. and C. Winston (Fontana Library of Theology and Philosophy, 1967).
Totem and Taboo, by S. Freud; trans. J. Strachey (Routledge and Kegan Paul, 1960).
The Psychology of Communication, by G. A. Miller (Penguin Books, 1970).
Fact and Fiction in Psychology, by H. J. Eysenck (Penguin Books, 1965).
Biblical quotations used in the book are from *The New English Bible*, published by the Oxford and Cambridge University Presses.

Index

Abott of Unreason, 15
abstract idea of number, 2
Adam, 47, 133
alchemy, 5
All-seeing Eye, 23
angels, 20, 165
anima, 12, 31, 134
Aphrodite, 12
Apostles, 23
Aquarius, 110
Arabs, 24, 65
Aries, 107
Aristotle, 50
arithmetic, 119
'as above, so below', 38, 97
Astarte, 13, 135
astrology, 103
Athensic, 56
awareness, 98, 144, 146
Aztecs, 55

Babel, Tower of, 161
Babylonians, 17, 55, 65, 69
Bacabs, 45
baktun, 25
Balaam, 22
Beast, Number of, 24
ben-ben, 8
Berossus, 56, 71
Bhagavad Gita, 35
Bible, 13, 44, 54, 74
binary arithmetic, 121
Bolivian myth, 55, 156
Brahmins, 29
Brazil, 56
Buddhists, 24, 30

Cabala, 66, 111
caduceus, 125, 133

calculation, 74, 87, 120
calendar
  Babylonian, 72
  Chinese, 75
  Mayan, 25
Calvary Cross, 100
Cancer, 108
candelabra, 21, 129
canopic jars, 45
Capricorn, 110
cards, playing, 118
caves, 165
Celebes Island myth, 157
celestial battles, 158
Celtic myth, 158
centre, 10, 41, 50, 84ff, 100, 102, 109
chakras, 127
chaos, 33, 54
Chinese, 24, 31, 54, 64, 75, 157
Christians, 9, 21, 30, 46
circle, 80, 84ff
colours, 26, 115
confession formula, 29
conjunctio oppositorum, 17, 108, 133
constellations, 106, 123
counting, 61ff, 87
creation, 2, 6, 11
  forces, 31
  myths, 53ff, 154ff
  principles, 53, 97, 139
  tablets, 55
Creator, 3, 15, 33, 52, 92, 98
cross, 6, 11, 46, 99, 101
crossroads, 99
crucifixion, 9, 44, 46, 99, 101

Darwin, 4
Deadly Sins, 19
death, 109

175

decimal system, 62
degrees, 82
Deluge, 31, 55, 155
Diana, 10
directions of space, 47, 76
divine year, 25
dreams, 11, 13, 22

Earth Mother, 8, 13, 55, 135
eclipse, 59, 167
Eden, 20, 39, 44, 109, 133, 148
Egyptians, 8, 29, 45, 52, 63, 79, 120, 160
elements, 6, 17, 44, 48, 59, 94, 96, 99, 103, 150
evolution, 39, 94ff

fall of man, 29
falling body, 164
falling rocks, 59, 168
Fates, 29
fertility, 131, 135
fire, 55, 163
First Cause, 48, 68
fish, symbol, 111
flood, 57, 150, 155, 163, 166, 172
four, 43ff
Frazer, 15, 131
Freud, Sigmund, 130, 138
Freya, Frigga, 7
Friday, 7, 14
Furies, 29

Garden of Eden, 20, 39, 109, 133, 148
gas, 95
Gemini, 107
Genesis, 15, 21, 39, 55, 66
Gilbert Island myth, 157
Gnostics, 113
Great Bear, 123
Great Work, 5
Great Year, 73
Graces, 29
Greeks, 24, 63
Guianan myth, 55
gunas, 35
Gurdjieff, 58

hand in numeration, 62
Hathor, 57, 160
heavens
    seven, 20

dividing, 88
heat, 95
Hebrews, 13, 21, 129
    alphabet, 112
Hecate, 10, 99
Heliopolis, 8
Hermes, 7, 12
    asteroid, 168
hermaphrodite, 12
Herodotus, 24
Hesperides, 24
hieroglyphics, 52
high priest, 38, 79
Hindus, 25, 35, 47, 74, 145
Hippocrates, 1
Horus, 45

Ichthus, 46
ikon, 49
immortality, 15
Indians, American, 56, 156
involution, 94ff
Isis, 45

Japanese
    gods of luck, 24
    legend, 157
Jehovah, 38, 112
Jericho, 22
Jews, 9, 37, 92
Jove, 7, 12
jubilee, 22
Jung, 12, 31, 45
Jupiter, 7, 12, 14

king-lists, 69
Kronos, 14

Leo, 108
Libra, 109
liquids, 95
Lord of Misrule, 15
Lord's Prayer, 20
Lot, 54, 160
lunation, 76

magic, 22, 38
Mahabharata, 73, 159
manvantara, 25
Mars, 7, 11, 14, 16
mathematics, 2, 61, 138
matter, 47, 94

INDEX

Mayas, 45, 62
mechanics, 32
menstrual cycle, 4
Mercury, 7, 12, 17, 115, 133
Moabites, 22
Mohammedans, 20, 127
Monday, 7
month, 80
moon
    goddesses of, 7, 10
    in creation myths, 57, 149
    phases of, 1, 4, 45, 81, 103
    second, 58, 149, 167, 172
mortality, 15
Muses, 29
music, 2

Neptune, 14, 29
Noah, 21, 54, 163
Nordic myth, 158
north, finding, 81
nudity, symbolic, 133
number
    abstract idea of, 2
    as symbol, 5
    masculine/feminine, 133

oath-taking, 24, 29
odd-man-out, 47, 97, 125
Odin, 7
On, 8
one, 3, 48
Orion, 123
Osiris, 45

paradox of sun symbol, 10
patriarch lists, 69, 171
perfection, 128, 140
Peru, 25
petitions of Lord's Prayer, 20
Pharaoh, 22
phases of moon, 1, 4, 45
Phoenicians, 13, 54, 160
pillars, 165
Pisces, 111
planes of existence, 25
planets, 5, 92, 105, 152
planetary gods, 5
Plato, 47
Platonic Year, 73
playing cards, 118
Pleiades, 123

plurality, 3
Pluto, 14
Plympton 322 tablet, 76
polarisation, 3, 11, 33, 44, 47, 101, 129
Polynesians, 54
Prajapatis, 25
precession of equinoxes, 73
principles of creation, 53, 97, 139, 140
psychic reality, 138
psychoanalysts, 51
psychological septenary, 136
psychological types, 44, 138
purpose, 143
pyramids, 8, 25, 52, 67, 101, 123
Pythagoreans, 2, 24, 29, 48, 66, 133
Pythagorean triangles, 76

quaternary, 43ff

Ra, 8, 57, 160
rainbow, 2, 26, 150
relativity, 50, 102
resurrection, 14
return to Source, 102
Revelation, Book of, 23, 44
Rhind Mathematical Papyrus, 120
right angle, 76
Rig Veda myth, 158
Rishis, 25
Romans, 63

Sabbath, 9, 22
sacraments, 20
sacrifice, 8, 11, 22, 24, 107, 109
Sagittarius, 110
Salome, 133
Saturday, 8, 14
Saturn, 8, 14
Saturnalia, 15
Scandinavians, 46
sciences, 19, 152
Scorpio, 109
seas, seven, 26
seasons, 10, 45, 81
selfhood, 98, 109
serpent, 39, 126
serpent-power, 127
Servers, seven, 23
seven
    ages of man, 26
    Baktuns, 25

-branched candelabra, 21, 129
chakras, 127
churches, 23
colours of rainbow, 26
days of week, 4ff
Deadly Sins, 19
eyes of the Lord, 23
gates of temple, 24
heavens, 20, 24, 127
Hesperides, 24
hills of Rome, 26
holes in saints' hearts, 24
Japanese gods, 24
at Jericho, 22
Kings at Thebes, 24
loaves, 23
Manus, 25
natural sciences, 19
notes in music, 24
and oath-taking, 24
pairs of animals in ark, 21
petitions of Lord's Prayer, 20
pillars of wisdom, 22
planes of existence, 25
Prajapatis, 25
in Revelation, 23
Rishis, 25
sacraments, 20
sacrifices, 22, 24
seas, 26
Servers, 23
sons and daughters of Niobe, 24
strings of Orpheus' lyre, 24
steps of *Bodhisatva*, 25
tails of fox, 24
and twelve, 6, 23, 28, 79
veils, dance of, 133
virtues, 19
wonders of world, 25
seventh
  day of seventh month, 24
  son of seventh son, 26
sex, 13, 17, 100, 109, 130
sexagesimal system, 74ff
shadow, 31
sins, deadly, 19
Sirius, 81
Sodom and Gomorrah, 149, 160
solids, 95
Solomon, 129
  Seal of, 37
Sothis, 81

Southern Cross, 123
Sphinx, 137
spiral, 39
square, 46, 67
stars, 2, 17, 105
Sumerians, 24, 126, 160
sun, 7, 8, 96, 103
  of Righteousness, 9
  symbolic, 16
Sunday, 7
swearing, 24, 29
symbol
  development of, 151
  manipulation of, 147
  and truth, 153
symbolic lists, 19

Tahiti myth, 158
Tarot, 111
tau cross, 47
Taurus, 107
ternary, 29ff
tetractys, 66
Tetragrammaton, 38, 112
thirteen, 1, 93
Thor, 7, 12
Thoth, 7
three
  -branched symbols of power, 29
  cult acts, 29
  denials of Peter, 29
  Fates and Furies, 29
  forces, 31
  gunas, 35
  heavenly bodies, 59
  wishes, 36
Thursday, 7, 12
tides, 4, 58, 167
Tiw, 7
Tree of Knowledge, 39, 55, 109, 126
Tree of Life, 39, 100, 111
triads, 30, 115
triangle, 33, 37, 66, 76, 140
Trinity, 11, 30, 36, 99, 101, 129
truth, 146
Tuesday, 7
twelve
  and alchemy, 6
  Apostles, 23
  houses of Zodiac, 79
  tribes of Israel, 79

INDEX

two, 48
"two-hand", 62

unity, concept of, 3

veneration, 13
Venus, 8, 13, 17, 115, 135
Virgo, 108, 135
virtues, 19
void, 33, 44, 54, 107
volcanoes, 59
Vulcan, 14

war, 11
Wednesday, 7

week, 4ff
Wheel of Life, 102
wisdom, pillars of, 23
wishes, three, 36
witchdoctors, 38
Woden, 7

Yahweh, 38
year, 80
yin-yang, 54, 131
yoga, 127

Zodiac, 79, 93, 102ff, 129
Zoroastrians, 31